JONES

Typing

First Course

THIRD EDITION

A. M. Drummond

Matthew Boulton Technical College, Birmingham

I. E. Scattergood

Formerly of British School of Commerce, Birmingham

McGRAW-HILL Book Company (UK) Limited

London · New York · St Louis · San Francisco · Auckland · Beirut · Bogotá · Düsseldorf
Johannesburg · Lisbon · Lucerne · Madrid · Mexico · Montreal · New Delhi · Panama
Paris · San Juan · São Paulo · Singapore · Sydney · Tokyo · Toronto

07 084212 4

Preface

The typewriter is the most commonly used business machine, and in the home it has become a popular writing instrument. For these reasons, more and more people are learning to type, and because of the thousands of students and teachers who have used the second edition of **Typing First Course** we felt it incumbent upon us to bring the text up to date. It is therefore with pleasure that we offer you the third edition of **Typing First Course** which is one book in a series of learning/teaching aids that will assist you to become an efficient typist.

The first series consists of:

Typing First Course which takes you well beyond the standard required for
(a) junior office typists;
(b) the elementary stage of any typewriting examination.

Keyboard Instruction Tapes—a series of tapes covering the presentation of the keyboard. These are suitable for
(a) individual practice at home or in the class-room;
(b) class teaching;
(c) reinforcement of keys previously practised.

Loose-Leaf Handbook and Solutions Manual which has sections dealing with
Skill Teaching
Syllabuses
Schemes of Work
Lesson Plans
Solutions to exercises in the main textbook
Programmed Learning Guides
Headed paper and forms which can be easily copied.

Practical Typing Exercises—Book One. This book contains further examples of exercises introduced in **Typing First Course**. Many of these exercises give the exact layout of typed documents and, therefore, are very easy to follow. Reference is made in **Typing First Course** to the relevant pages in **Practical Typing Exercises.**

The purpose of **Typing First Course** is to help you
(a) acquire smooth and correct finger movement;
(b) raise the level and broaden the foundation of the skills and techniques practised in (a); and
(c) apply the skills and techniques to practical work.

If you play a musical instrument, swim, or play tennis, you will know that it takes patience and practice to master the skills involved in any of these activities, and, also, that the more expert you wish to become, the harder you must practise. The same applies when learning to type. At first your fingers will not move very quickly but, before long, you will find that they will move faster and faster as your control of the keys becomes more and more automatic, provided good work habits and correct techniques are maintained from the beginning and practised continuously.

You will welcome the special features of this new edition:

Large typeface for keyboard drills.
Where desired, quicker completion of the keyboard.

Twenty-minute lessons—in the keyboard learning stage, each unit can be covered in 20 minutes.

Fully-blocked style in tabulation.
Greater concentration on metric measurements.
Up-to-date content—most exercise material is completely new.

In addition, this textbook retains all the popular features of the previous editions that students and teachers found helpful:

Two-colours to enable a 'visual' presentation of all new keys.
The second colour also emphasizes styling and display both in the text and in the form of marginal reminders.

Skill-building drills, accuracy and speed practice are a built-in, essential part of the course.

Explanations, points of theory, and specimens of all new work are short and simple to understand.
Specimens are displayed as they should appear when typed.
All production work (there are 60 Production Jobs) has a timed target based on the average times taken by students of varying ability.

Flexibility is provided by the separation of keyboard techniques, accuracy/speed practice, new work, and office production typing.

Back-spacing method of centring tabulation.

Seven consolidation units—each unit contains exercises on all the work covered up to that particular unit.

Test material—16 Production Jobs—covering all aspects of office- and examination-style typing.

Keyboard Coverage

Alphabet keys. Since the publication of the second edition, we have had innumerable requests for quicker keyboard coverage, and, while we agree that this is advantageous for some students, we must also say that not everyone can learn the keyboard successfully at a quick pace. To cover the needs of all learners, we have:

(a) Introduced only two alphabet keys in each unit. As in the previous editions, after the introduction of the home keys, only one new key is presented at a time.

(b) Given only two lines of drills on each new key. These drills are very easy, consisting mainly of words of three letters.

(c) After introducing the two new keys, given a further two lines of WORD FAMILY drills on these keys.

(d) As in previous editions, at the beginning of each keyboard unit, given three lines of REVIEW THE KEYS YOU KNOW and at the end of each unit three lines of APPLY THE KEYS YOU KNOW.

(e) For students who prefer to spend a little more time on the alphabet keys, included three IMPROVEMENT PRACTICE UNITS—8, 12, and 18—each with two pages of drills on the keys introduced prior to the particular unit.

Twenty-minute modules. A number of schools and colleges are now switching to computer scheduling, open-plan classrooms, individualized instruction etc., and to meet the needs of the old and the new, the units covering the keyboard learning stages have been planned so that each unit can be completed in 20 minutes—the exceptions are the IMPROVEMENT PRACTICE UNITS. This means that, if you do not need to use the IMPROVEMENT PRACTICE UNITS, you will complete the alphabet keyboard in 5 hours.

Large typeface. All drills covering the alphabet keyboard are printed in large typeface which is easily read letter by letter at arm's length.

Figures and special characters. The figures and special characters are presented in Units 25–35: the special characters are introduced immediately after the presentation of the relevant figure key. In these 11 Units there is a sequence of:

(a) Alphabet reviews which provide ample keyboard revision and practice.

(b) Intensive drills on figures and special characters.

(c) Accuracy and speed practice.

(d) Introduction of, and intensive practice on, display work and line-end division.

Skill Building and Technique Development

From Unit 37 onwards, accuracy, speed, new work and production work are developed in a carefully balanced sequence of activities:

(a) Skill Building
   i. Keyboard Techniques
   ii. Accuracy or Speed Practice
   iii. Record Your Progress
(b) Technique Development (New work)
(c) Production Typing.

Skill Building Units
 i. *Keyboard Technique.* Each unit starts with an alphabetic sentence which is an excellent warm-up drill and at the same time gives intensive practice on the alphabet keys: this in turn improves accuracy. There then follow keyboard reviews which include the following drills: fluency, phrase, hyphen, line-end division, one-hand word, space bar, figure, punctuation, word family, shift key, special character, carriage return, vowel, prefix, suffix, double letter, etc.
 ii. *Accuracy or speed practice.* **Typing First Course** contains a complete programme of accuracy/speed practice. The passages start in Unit 19 at 19 w.p.m. (one-minute timing) and progress in easy stages to 30 w.p.m.

(one-minute timing) in Unit 63. From Unit 63, the length of the 30 w.p.m. passages is graduated in ¾ minutes to 2 minutes in Unit 68.

From Unit 72, the length of the 30 w.p.m. *accuracy* passages is graduated in ¾ minutes to a maximum of 6½ minutes in Unit 93. Because it is easier to build speed on short (2 minutes or less) easy passages, the *speed* building material is given separately from Unit 72. In this unit the speed passages start at 35 w.p.m. for one minute and move in easy stages to 45 w.p.m. for 2 minutes in Unit 93. Whether you practise for accuracy or speed is a very personal matter and can only be decided by you or on advice from your teacher. Accuracy is the result of correct practice combined with good techniques, good posture, and correct reading of copy. Speed, without any thought of accuracy, will lead only to fast but inaccurate typing.

As a guide, we suggest that you work for accuracy if you have more than one error for each minute typed. If you have one error or less for each minute typed, then you may aim for a slight increase in speed. You should work up to the desired speed gradually and, having reached the speed, practice should continue at that speed until the required standard of accuracy is reached.

iii. Record Your Progress. There are 31 Record Your Progress exercises. The exercises are printed in Pica type face and the object is to let you know how you are progressing when typing from straight copy. A Record Your Progress Chart is given in the Handbook and Solutions Manual.

Syllabic Intensity (Copy control). We believe that a controlled but random and unselected vocabulary is the most effective way of building typing skills and, therefore, the difficulty of the copy in Accuracy, Speed, and Record Your Progress exercises has been graded according to the syllabic intensity. Syllabic intensity means the average number of syllables in the words of a passage. Thus in Accuracy/Speed Practice AS.4 (page 29) S.I. 1.09 means that there is an average of 1.09 syllables per word.

Technique development units introduce new work in small and easy specific steps. The first exercise on all new work is set out clearly, and the essential features are emphasized in the second colour.

Manuscript. Typing from manuscript has been introduced immediately after display work (Unit 42) because many typists, particularly in their first job, are called upon to copy from handwritten drafts.

Business letters. We have concentrated on fully-blocked letters with open punctuation because:

(a) it simplifies the initial approach to business letters;

(b) it is being used increasingly in business;

(c) it is now accepted by examining bodies as a form of layout.

Business letters in semi-block style, and standard punctuation, have been included. To avoid confusion these have been separated. Decide on the style with which you wish to start and practise that style intensively before moving on to another style.

Tabulation. Blocked tabulation is quite acceptable in business and by most examining bodies. Ample practice is given in both centred and blocked styles of tabulation.

Production Typing. Typing First Course is as much concerned with applying typing skill as with building it. Production typing is introduced only when your speed and accuracy standards and the machine techniques necessary for reasonably fast output have been acquired. The inclusion of timed production targets emphasizes the importance of accuracy, speed, theory, and good machine techniques in all typing.

Other Features

Review Quizzes. The Review Quizzes afford a thorough and rapid recall of punctuation, display and theory. Self-checking answers are included at the end of the text.

Secretarial Aids. The Secretarial Aids give useful information for the office typist about:

1. Books of Reference.
2. Getting Letters ready for the Post.
3. Opening and Distributing the Post.

4. Office Stationery.
5. Typing Postcards and Memoranda.
6. Checking Appointments.

Loose-leaf Handbook and Solutions Manual.

Part I contains:

1. A brief explanation of how TYPING FIRST COURSE was planned so that it incorporates a complete and systematic skill-building plan. There are also hints on how to use the textbook.
2. A brief but concise review of the basic principles of how typing skill is acquired and developed.
3. Syllabuses and Schemes of Work for full- and part-time courses, and helpful suggestions on how to plan a lesson.
4. Ideas on the presentation of a lesson.

Part II contains:

1. Each unit of TYPING FIRST COURSE is reviewed and suggestions given for lesson presentation.
2. All exercises not set out in the main text are displayed as they should look when typed. These examples give margin and tab stops together with calculations for horizontal and vertical display.
3. As the book is loose-leaf, students' record sheets (Technique Check List, Record Your Progress Chart, etc.) and printed letter headings, invoice forms, form letters, etc., may be copied and duplicated.
4. Learning Guides—these will not only train students to type accurately and quickly, but also train them in
   (a) the efficient use of the complete machine; and
   (b) the automatic application of typing theory which is essential to all typists.

Acknowledgments

The exercises in the book have been tested under practical conditions over the past few years by many teachers to whom we are indebted for their suggestions and criticisms concerning the suitability of the material included and the timing of production exercises. We also wish to thank our colleagues for the help given in copying the manuscript exercises.

We sincerely hope that you have enjoyed working through the first series of books and aids and that you will now proceed to

Second Series:

Applied Typing presents a systematic and comprehensive programme for perfecting and applying typing skill up to the standard of the intermediate and advanced stages of any typing examination.

Loose-Leaf Solutions Manual gives solutions to all exercises not displayed in APPLIED TYPING and headed paper and forms which can be copied easily.

Practical Typing Exercises—Book Two. This book contains further examples of exercises introduced in **Applied Typing**. Many of these exercises give the exact layout of typed documents and, therefore, are easy to follow. Reference is made in **Applied Typing** to the relevant pages in **Practical Typing Exercises**.

A. M. Drummond
I. E. Scattergood

Index to Contents

Type an original and two copies of the following. Use A4 paper, single spacing, and block paragraphs unless otherwise instructed.

At a meeting of Management & Staff Representatives held on 22nd Aug., 1977, the following matters were discussed.

Annual Leave.   It was agreed that entitlement to additional leave should be related to years of completed service whether or not there had been a break *in the service*   *after 10 years' service*

Mileage Allowance.   It was agreed that the mileage allowance as set out in Section IV of the handbook should be applied to all staff who used their cars for business purposes.   Threshold Payments.   The Secretary pointed out that these would be consolidated into the salary scales as from 1 Sept 77. *payments*

Overtime. As from 1st Oct 1977, where any employee is required to work in excess of 35 hours a week, then the following options should apply:

(i) time off in lieu should be given wherever possible; or where this is not possible

Hanging paras please

(ii) payment should be made at the rate of time and a half if the *double time* work was performed on week days, and if the work was carried out on Saturdays, Sundays, or during Statutory holidays.

cost of Living.

The staff representatives submitted that the increases in the cost of living was such that it had now eroded the increase given in January of this year and that a further increase was now necessary.   Management replied that the cost of living index had not moved a sufficient number of points to have overtaken the increase, but promised to keep the Index under constant ~~super~~ revision. *to keep pace w. the cost of living*

Retirement.   It was agreed that Management provide facilities to enable staff, within two years of their expected date of retirement, to make proper preparation for retirement.   Employees are to be given special pay to attend courses organised by Local Colleges of Further Education. *leave with*   *Typist - Please insert main heading:* STAFF NOTICE *(spaced caps)*

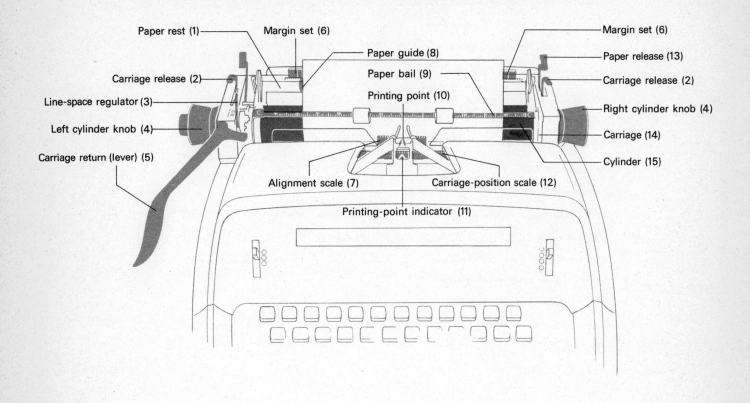

Paper rest (1)
Margin set (6)
Paper guide (8)
Paper bail (9)
Printing point (10)
Margin set (6)
Paper release (13)
Carriage release (2)
Carriage release (2)
Line-space regulator (3)
Right cylinder knob (4)
Left cylinder knob (4)
Carriage (14)
Carriage return (lever) (5)
Cylinder (15)
Alignment scale (7)
Carriage-position scale (12)
Printing-point indicator (11)

1. 'Paper rest' . . . the paper rests on it . . . so does the paper guide.

2. 'Carriage release' . . . frees carriage so it can be moved easily by hand to right or left . . . one at each end of the carriage. When you depress it, hold the adjacent cylinder knob firmly.

3. 'Line-space regulator' . . . controls the distance that the paper turns up when the carriage is returned by key or lever.

4. 'Cylinder or Platen knob' . . . the large knob at each end of the cylinder.

5. 'Carriage return' . . . used to return the carriage and to space up the paper for the start of a new line of typing. On electrics, it is a large key at the right-hand side of the keyboard instead of the lever shown in the drawing.

6. 'Margin sets' . . . devices used to adjust the margin stops that control the width of the margin on each side of the paper.

7. 'Alignment scale' . . . close to the cylinder behind the ribbon on each side of the printing point. Indicates the exact writing line.

8. 'Paper guide' . . . used to guide the paper uniformly into the carriage.

9. 'Paper bail' . . . clamps the paper against the cylinder . . . must be raised or pulled forward when you insert or straighten your paper.

10. 'Printing point' . . . the V-shaped slot where the type bars come up to strike and print on the paper.

11. 'Printing-point indicator' . . . a line or mark or arrowhead

pointing to the space on the carriage-position scale to which the carriage has moved and at which the machine is ready to print.

12. 'Carriage-position scale' . . . counts the spaces across the cylinder.

13. 'Paper release' . . . loosens the paper for straightening or removal.

14. 'Carriage' . . . the top, movable part of the machine . . . carries the paper . . . moves horizontally to right and left.

15. 'Cylinder or Platen' . . . the long roller in the carriage around which the paper turns . . . paper and cylinder turn each time you return the carriage or turn one of the cylinder knobs.

ESSENTIAL MACHINE PARTS

Type the following letter on A4 paper. Mark letter for the
attention of H Griffiths, Esq. Take one carbon copy and
address an envelope. Insert today's date.

Our ref WM/DES

William Griffiths & Co

18 City Road

Haverfordwest   Dyfed   SA61 1AA

Dear Sirs

Thank you for yr enquiry.

NP/   We hv sent to you under separate cover our catalogues
covering Office Furniture & Filing Equipment. [We hv
pleasure in attaching details of our leasing facilities
uc/   for Office Furniture.

Yrs ffy

The Universal Supply Co Ltd

W Mills

Sales Dept

Job 59   Production Target—twelve minutes

Type the following on a sheet of A5 landscape paper in
single-line spacing. Use block paragraphs.

TELEX SERVICE

The PO Telex Service provides a fast means of
printed communication – the sender & the receiver each
hv a typed copy of a message sent by teleprinter. A
teleprinter has a keyboard similar to th of a typewriter,
particular & to send a message to a organisation, dial the telex
μ no. of th organ. If the line is free, you wl be
connectd. The sender then types the message on her
teleprinter & it is typed automatically, at the same time,
on the receiver's teleprinter.

Extra Equipment) Details of automatic transmitters,
receivers, & perforators are available from the PO.

Telex Directories. Subscribers are supplied w a free
uc   copy of the U.K Telex directory.

Shoulder headings, please   Typist – Abbreviations
in full

1.

2.

1. Check the position of the paper guide

One of the marks on the paper rest shows where to set the paper guide so that the left edge of the paper will be at '0' on the carriage-position scale. Check that the paper guide is set at that mark.

2. Set the line-space regulator for single spacing

The line-space regulator has a *1*, a *2*, and a *3* printed on or beside it. Adjust the regulator so that it is in the *1* position. In addition, many machines are now fitted with half-line spacing to give 1½ and 2½ line-spaces. Examine your machine and check the line-spacing.

3. Set the margins as indicated in each unit or exercise

(a) On some machines you can see the margin stops on the front of the carriage, or behind the paper rest. On such machines: (1) press the button on top of the stop, (2) slide the stop to the point you wish, and (3) then release the button.

(b) On other machines you cannot see the margin stops. You must use a margin-set key. You may have a separate margin-set key at each end of the carriage, or you may have one key on the keyboard for use with both stops. On such machines: (1) move the carriage to the present setting of the stop, (2) press the margin-set key while you move the carriage to the point where you want the margin, and (3) then release the set key.

(c) In the keyboard learning stage (pages 5–31) only the left margin need be set. From page 32 onwards set margins at scale-points given.

As you progress through the textbook, you will find instructions such as 'Use suitable margins'—in such cases you must decide what margins to use. What is important is that, in the majority of exercises other than display and tabulation, your left margin must be wider than your right margin, e.g., Elite 22–82 (there are 22 clear spaces on the left and 18 clear spaces on the right).

In other cases you may be given measurements for your margins, e.g., 25 mm (one inch) on left and 13 mm (half an inch) on the right. This would mean that, when using A4 paper, you would have margins of Elite 12–94, Pica 10–77. With Elite type there are 12 spaces to 25 mm and with Pica type there are 10 spaces to 25 mm.

4.

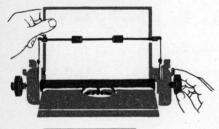

4. Get the paper bail out of the way

Pull the paper bail forward or up, temporarily away from the cylinder, so that you may insert paper without its bumping into the paper bail.

5.

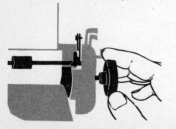

5. Insert a sheet of paper

Hold the sheet in your left hand. Place the paper behind the cylinder, against the raised edge of the paper guide. Turn the right cylinder knob to draw the paper into the machine.

To prevent damage to the cylinder of the typewriter, use a backing sheet such as is usually supplied in boxes of carbon paper, or use a sheet of stout paper.

6.

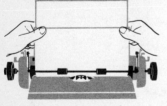

6. Check that the paper is straight

Push the top of the paper back. If the left side of the paper, at both top and bottom, fits evenly against the paper guide, your paper is straight. If it is not straight, loosen the paper (use the paper release), straighten it, and return the paper release to its normal position.

7. Place the paper bail against the paper

Slide the rubber rollers on the bail to the right or left to divide the paper into thirds. Then, set the bail back against the paper.

8.

8. Adjust the paper for the top margin

(a) When typing drills, turn the paper back, using the right cylinder knob, until only a small portion of paper shows above the paper bail.

(b) When typing production exercises (apart from display and tabulation) the majority of exercises typed on plain paper start on the seventh single-line space from the top edge of the paper, which means you leave 6 spaces (25 mm or one inch) clear. To do this proceed as follows:

i. Insert paper
ii. Check to see that paper is straight (see 6 above)
iii Turn paper back so that top edge is level with top edge of alignment scale (See page 1 No. 7).
iv. Turn up 7 single-line spaces.

PREPARING TO TYPE

Examiner's Report (Centre in caps & u/score)

SHORTHAND
80 w.p.m. ʒ/   Abt. a quarter of the candidates produced perfect scripts/ a quarter failed; and of the remainder a ¼ passed in spite of their s'hand.

serious /   Spelling still causes/difficulty. Unfortunately candidates do not seem to realise th. they

ʒ/   cannot spell and/ therefore/ do not make use of the dictionaries provided. ⌐

run on/   I must again point out th. a sh-typist who cannot spell is a liability to any organisation.

TYPING
(Stage II)
   Most candidates completed all the questions and, on the whole, the scripts were very satisfactory.

most/   The/common error was the omission of ballooned matter, and it was obvious that candidates had

carefully /   not bothered to read the questions/ before typing.

ʋ́ ʋ̈ ʋ̈   Candidates are advised to make full use of the 10 minutes/ reading time/ wh. is now allowed before typing starts.

SECRETARIAL
DUTIES
(Stage II)
   A surprising no. of candidates failed to reach the required standard because:

(a) They did not answer the question. They answered a question given last year on the same topic/ ⊙

Although this paper was a little more difficult than usual, there were some v. gd. scripts.

uc/   (b) they were unable to apply their knowledge to specific situations.

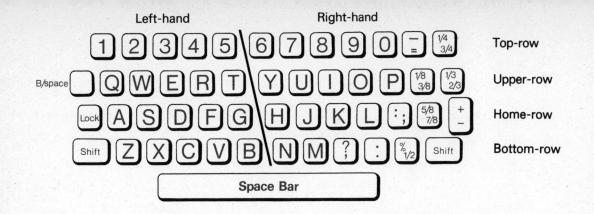

The ready-to-type position

1. Place your book on the right-hand side of your machine, or as indicated by your teacher.
2. Place your finger tips on the home keys: Left finger tips on A S D F and right finger tips on J K L ;. Check that you placed them correctly.
3. Keep your **left** thumb close to your left first finger.
4. Extend your right thumb so that it is slightly above the centre of the space bar.
5. Now, check your posture.
    Your head—hold it erect, facing the book.
    Your shoulders—hold them back, and relaxed.
    Your body—centre yourself opposite the J-key a hand-span away from the machine.
    Your back—sit erect, with your body sloping slightly forward from the hips.
    Arms and elbows—let them hang loosely.
    Wrists—keep them low, barely clearing the machine.
    Hands—close together, low, flat across the backs.
    Fingers—curved as though to grasp a handle bar.
    Waist—sit back in the chair.
    Knees—keep them apart. Do **not**, ever, cross them.
    Feet—place them apart, braced firmly on the floor.

The space bar

With the right thumb, **tap** the space bar. **Bounce** the thumb off the space bar. Keep your other fingers still, on their home keys.

Return the carriage

Manual Machines. To return the carriage for a new line, you must use the carriage-return lever. With one quick sweep of your hand and forearm, you must combine these four motions:

1. Your left hand starts up towards the carriage-return lever.
2. You put the first finger and next finger or two against the lever.
3. With a twist of your wrist, you *toss* the carriage back.
4. Return your left hand to its home position.

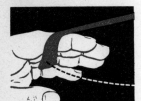

Electric Machines. In one quick motion you—

1. Raise the little finger of the right hand and *stab* the return key that is at the right-hand end of the keyboard.
2. Return the little finger to its home key immediately.

CORRECT TYPING POSTURE

3

Our ref. DP/LC.

TYPIST:
Please insert current year.

Dear Sir (s), <u>OFFICE SUPPLIES</u>

Our catalogues will be ready for mailing at the end of this month. There are 4 catalogues, ea. covering one of the following sections:

OFFICE MACHINES   OFFICE FURNITURE
FILING EQUIPMENT   STATIONERY & ACCESSORIES

Because of rising inflation, many organisations now lease machines, equipment, and furniture, lease rentals do not fluctuate as these are fixed for the period of the lease, and leasing periods vary in between three and 6 years. [Please complete the tear off portions of this letter and send it to us. We shall be happy to send y. complete details of and, should you wish it, our rep. will be pleased to call and see y.

at the bottom

Yrs. ffy.
THE UNIVERSAL SUPPLY Co. LTD.

- -

To: The Universal Supply Co. Ltd.,
84-88 High Street, Aberdeen AB2 3HE.

NAME ....
ADDRESS ....
....Postcode ....

Please send the following catalogues.
(Underline the ones you require)

OFFICE MACHINES   OFFICE FURNITURE
FILING EQUIPMENT   STATIONERY & ACCESSORIES

Also, please let me have details of your leasing facilities for: (Underline the one(s) about which you require further information.)

OFFICE MACHINES   OFFICE FURNITURE   FILING EQUIPMENT

A S D F

J K L ;

Space Bar

Left thumb close to first finger

Right thumb above space bar

Check your posture—page 3.

Check insertion of paper, line spacing and margin sets—page 2.

Place fingers on home keys—see above.

Finger Movement

1. Without typing, practise the finger movement for each exercise. During this preliminary practice you may look at your fingers. You will find it helpful to say the letters aloud. Continue this preliminary practice until your fingers 'know' where to move from the home key. Always return finger to its home key.

2. When you are confident that your fingers have acquired the correct movement, repeat this practice *without looking at your fingers*. Keep your eyes on the copy in your book, and do not strike the keys. If you hesitate in making the finger movement, repeat step one.

3. Practise the finger movement for each new key until your finger moves confidently and crisply to that key.

Striking the keys

1. Let your finger bounce off each key and return to home key.

2. Reach with finger only; do *not* move wrist or arm.

3. For manual machines, strike key firmly and sharply; for electric machine, stroke key.

4. Strike keys, including space bar, evenly—one for each 'tick' and one for each 'tock' of the clock.

Relax

Notice the natural and relaxed posture of the typist on page 3. Avoid all strain and tension when you are typing. Let your movement be smooth and easy.

CORRECT TYPING TECHNIQUE

Type a copy of the following exercise on A4 paper. Where items are numbered
in small roman numerals, please use hanging paragraphs where appropriate.

DUPLICATING PROCESSES

I *X*. STENCIL

   The master is cut by typewriter or in longhand by
tl means of a s*t*ylus pen.   STYLUS

   Advantages

easily i. Corrections are made (correcting fluid is used) *O*
       ii. Good quality reproduction *O*
      iii. Up to 7,000 copies can be run off from one master.
       iv. Masters may be stored and used again.
        v. Masters may be made by photographic process.

II *2*. SPIRIT

   A special type of paper backed by a carbon is used
21 ~~to prepare~~ in preparing the master which may be
   typed in the usual way. *or written*

   Advantages

        i. One or several colours may be included in the
            same master. (by using different coloured carbons) *lly*
bel ii. Masters may very easily prepared.
used iii. Paper for copies is of better quality than that in
            stencil duplicating.

III *3*. OFFSET LITHOGRAPHY
                          or written
   Master may be typed but a special grease based ribbon *H*
   (or pencil) must be used.

   Advantages

   1. Quality of reproduction is very high.
   2. Much cheaper than printing & results almost as
       gd.
   3. Any type of paper may be used f. copies.
   4. A good quality master will produce up to 50,000 copies.
   5. Masters are often prepared by photographic process.

A. Set margins and insert paper

1. Set left margin at 30 Elite, 22 Pica

2. Set paper guide at '0'

3. Set line-space regulator at '1'

4. Raise paper bail bar out of the way

5. (a) Take a sheet of A4 paper in your left hand
   (b) Place the paper behind the cylinder with the left edge against the raised edge of the paper guide
   (c) With your right hand turn the right cylinder knob clockwise to draw the paper into the machine

6. Check that paper is straight by pushing the top of the paper back. If top and bottom of paper do not fit evenly against the paper guide
   (a) Use paper release to loosen paper
   (b) Straighten paper
   (c) Return paper release lever to normal position

7. Return paper bail to normal position

8. Turn the paper back, using right cylinder knob, until only a small portion of paper shows above paper bail

B. Ready-to-type position

1. Place book on right-hand side of machine

2. Feet—place them apart, braced firmly on the floor

3. Arms and elbows—let them hang loosely

4. Fingers: (a) place left-hand fingers on ASDF
   (b) right-hand fingers on JKL;
   (c) curve fingers as though to grasp a handle bar
   (d) practise looking at the keyboard and placing your fingers on the HOME KEYS—ASDF JKL;
   (e) *never* type while looking at the keyboard

5. Sit back and relax

C. In a few seconds you will type the exercise in 'D' below, but, before you start, remember that when STRIKING THE KEYS

MANUAL MACHINE—strike key firmly and sharply
ELECTRIC MACHINE—stroke key

D. 1. Push carriage to right so that it stops at left margin

   2. Look at the keyboard and place your left-hand fingers on ASDF and right-hand fingers on JKL;

   3. Type the following line exactly as it stands—keeping your eyes on textbook

   4. fffjjjfffjjjfffjjjfffjjjfffjjjfffjjjfffj

   5. Sit back and relax for a few seconds

Type an original and two copies of the following letter. Mark the letter for the attention of Mrs. P. G. Barker. On the top left-hand corner of the first carbon copy type: Mr. J. R. Nicholson—for information.

Your ref. PGB/PB Our ref. WM/BC

19th May, 1977

R. MacGregor & Co. Ltd.,
18 Commercial Str.,
PETERHEAD, Aberdeenshire. AB4 6AA

Dear Sirs,

<u>PRINTING CALCULATORS</u>

Thank you for yr enquiry dated 16th May.

The following is our quotation f. the 2 calculators abt which y. enquired:

1021 J Electronic Printing Calculator, 10 digit
capacity, constant & memory - - - - - - - £208.00

1033 J Electronic Printing Calculator,
12 digit capacity, constant, 2
memories and % key - - - - - - - £315.00

The above prices are subject to VAT, & dly will be ex stock.

Please do not hesitate to tel. if you require further information.

Yrs ffy

The Universal Supply Co. Ltd.

W. Mills
Sales Dept.

These m/cs are guaranteed for twelve months, 3 months labour, 12 months parts.

E. Carriage return

1. MANUAL MACHINES

(a) Preliminary practice *without returning the carriage.* Look at the carriage return lever and raise your *left hand* and put the first finger and next finger or two against the lever. Practise the movement from the HOME KEYS to carriage return lever and back to HOME KEYS.

(b) Right- and left-hand fingers on HOME KEYS.

(c) Right-hand fingers remain on JKL;.

(d) With eyes on textbook
   (i) raise left hand and, with a twist of the wrist, toss the carriage back
   (ii) return left hand to ASDF.

2. ELECTRIC MACHINES

(a) Preliminary practice *without returning the carriage.* Look at the carriage return key (on the right-hand side of the keyboard) and make the reach with your right-hand little finger from the semicolon to the return key and back to semicolon.

(b) All fingers remain just slightly above their HOME KEY except right-hand little finger.

(c) With eyes on textbook
   (i) raise the little finger of the right hand and stab the return key
   (ii) return little finger to semicolon key immediately.

F. You are now going to type lines numbered 1 and 2 below. When you have typed the line numbered 1, you must return the carriage immediately without looking up from textbook and then start typing line numbered 2. (Do not type the numbers.)

1. fffjjjfffjjjfffjjjfffjjjfffjjjfffjjjfffj

   Return carriage

2. fffjjjfffjjjfffjjjfffjjjfffjjjfffjjjfffj

   Return carriage twice and look at what you have typed

G. Space Bar

A clear space is left between each group of letters or words. This is done by striking the space bar with the *right thumb.* Keep your other fingers on the home keys as you bounce the thumb off the space bar. Type the following line three times.

3. fff jjj fff jjj fjf jfj fff jjj fff fjfj

(a) Type an original and one copy of the following requisition form on A5 portrait paper.

<u>STATIONERY REQUISITION</u>

DEPARTMENT   DATE

Please supply

Quantity	Item

38 mm (1½")   *76 mm (3")*

Authorised _____

HEAD OF DEPARTMENT

Received the above items _____

(b) On the carbon copy insert the following details.

Dept — Sales   Today's date
  4 reams   A4 Duplicating Paper (white)
  3 "   A4 Bank Typing Paper
  1 box   A4 Carbon Paper
  1 roll   Sellotape   S/

(c) On original insert:

Dept — Purchasing   Today's date
  6   HB Pencils
  3   Biro Pens (red)
  2 reams   A5 Bond Headed Paper
  2 boxes   Paper Clips
  3   Scrap Pads

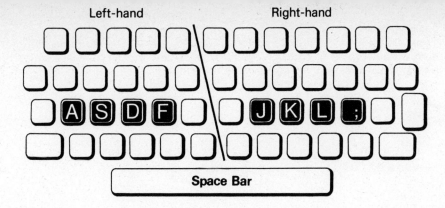

Type each line or sentence three times, saying the letters to yourself. If time permits, complete your practice by typing each group of lines as it appears. Keep your eyes on the copy and return the carriage sharply. Set left margin stop at 30 Elite, 22 Pica.

A. Practise F and J keys—First fingers

Keep other fingers on home keys

1. fff jjj fjf jfj fjf jfj fff jjj fff fjfj

Always turn up twice between exercises

B. Practise D and K keys—Second fingers

Raise first fingers slightly. Keep little fingers on home keys

2. ddd kkk dkd kdk dkd kdk ddd kkk dkd dkdk

3. fff jjj ddd kkk fkf kfk jdj djd fjk fdjk

Use an even stroke for space bar

C. Practise S and L keys—Third fingers

Raise little fingers over home keys. Keep first fingers on home keys

4. sss lll sls lsl sls lsl sss lll sls slsl

5. fff jjj ddd kkk sss lll fds jkl fds jklj

Feet firmly on floor

D. Practise A and ; keys—Little fingers

Keep first fingers on home keys

6. aaa ;;; a;a ;a; a;a ;a; aaa ;;; ;a; a;a;

7. f;f jaj d;d kak a;s lal aaa ;;; a;a a;a;

E. Word-building

8. aaa lll all lll aaa ddd lad ddd aaa dad;

9. fff aaa ddd fad sss aaa ddd sad fad lad;

F. Apply the keys you know

10. all sad lads; a sad lass; a lad asks dad

11. all sad lads ask a dad; a sad lass falls

12. as a lass falls dad falls; all lads fall

One space after semicolon

Type a copy of the following exercise on A4 paper. Use suitable margins and single spacing. The numbers should be typed at the left margin, and the paragraphs blocked five spaces from the margin.

Caps and underscore ——→ General Hints and Examination Reminders

each

1. Always read carefully all instruction for exercise before you begin to type.

3 2. Mark in pencil the points at which any insertions are to be made so that you do not forget them ~~when you reach these points~~.

stet 4. Use common-sense in deciphering manuscript and also the arrange- *in* ment of matter when this has to be continued on a second page.

or tabulated matter,

5 4. If you are not sure how to set out any manuscript it is a good plan to follow the setting ~~given~~ unless, of course, other instructions are

N.P. given. [*5.6* When any part of a letter or manuscript is to be inset see that you centre it in the typing line, so that equal space is left on either side of the inset portion. *tro.*

(of the original)

2 6. Do not be satisfied with slipshod work; correct neatly any typing errors before removing your paper from the machine.

(Never in any circumstances shd you overtype.)

H 7. When deciding on margins, remember that the right hand margin
H   should never be greater than the left hand margin.

8. In tabular work, take care to centre the matter vertically as well as horizontally and also see that the columns are of a suitable width for the matter to be inserted.

9. It is absolutely essential that you should be consistent when a date occurs again in the same piece of work it must be typed in the

u.c. same way not June 2 or 2 june. *(, i.e.,)*

Run on Also if any item of figures contains two figures after the decimal point, there must always be 2 figures in every item, e.g., £3.00.

(, e.g., if the date is typed first as 4th June, 1977,)

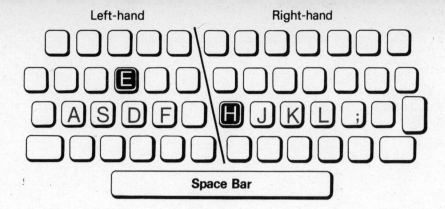

Left-hand   Right-hand

Space Bar

Type each line or sentence three times, saying the letters to yourself. If time permits, complete your practice by typing each group of lines as it appears. Keep your eyes on the copy and return the carriage sharply. Set left margin stop at 30 Elite, 22 Pica.

A.   Review the keys you know

1. aaa ;;; sss lll ddd kkk fff jjj asd jkl;   Return carriage without looking up

2. ask a lad; ask all lads; ask a sad lass;

3. all lads fall; dad falls; dad asks a lad

Turn up twice between exercises

B.   Practise E key—D finger

Practise D to E back to D. Keep other fingers on home keys

4. ddd eee ded ded see ded lee ded fee ded;

5. ded sea ded lea ded led ded fed ded eke;

C.   Practise H key—J finger

Practise J to H back to J. Keep other fingers on home keys

6. jjj hhh jhj jhj has jhj had jhj she jhj;

7. jhj has jhj had jhj she jhj ash jhj dash

D.   Practise word-building

8. hhh eee lll ddd held jjj aaa fff jaffas;

9. sss hhh aaa lll shall fff eee ddd feeds;

E.   Apply the keys you know

10. a lass has had a salad; dad sees a lake;   Use right thumb and even stroke for space bar

11. a jaffa salad; she held a sale; he shall

12. she feeds a lad; dad has a hall; a shed;

UNIT 3   **8**

Type the following statement of account on a suitable form.

From: The Universal Supply Co. Ltd., 84-114 High Street,
      Aberdeen.   AB2 3HE
To: John Jones & Co., 45 Thomas Street, Liverpool.   L1 6BJ
FO. 189   Terms: Nett 30 days

1977

May			Balance			48.50
June	1	4891	Goods	90.15		138.65
	6	4956	Goods	24.25		162.90
	10		Returns		10.15	152.75
	14		Cheque		38.35	114.40
	17	5172	Goods	105.40		219.80
	23	5284	Goods	423.35		643.15
	28		Cheque		90.15	553.00

Job 51   Production Target—eighteen minutes

Display the following table on paper of a suitable size. Use leader dots and rule.

CARAVAN SALE

Name	No. of Berths	Size[1]	Price[2]
Europa	2	2.75 x 1.50	£ 2,000
Rowan	4	3.00 x 2.00	2,325
Scotia	4	3.75 x 2.00	2,400
Daffodil	4	4.25 x 1.50	2,375
Night	4	3.75 x 2.00	2,425
Dawn	4	4.25 x 2.00	2,475 ~~2,475~~ 50
The Favourite	2	4.75 x 2.00	~~3,000~~ 2,500
~~The~~ Mink	~~3~~4	4.75 x 2.00	2,600
Panorama	4	5.00 x 2.00	2,750

(1) In metres

(2) Does not include VAT

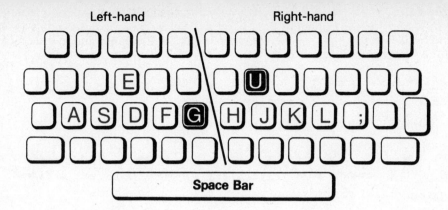

Space Bar

Type each line or sentence three times, saying the letters to yourself. If time permits, complete your practice by typing each group of lines as it appears. Keep your eyes on the copy and return the carriage sharply. Set left margin stop at 30 Elite, 22 Pica.

A.   Review the keys you know

1. asd ;lk ded jhj def khj fed has lee had;   Wrists and arms
                                                  straight
2. add salads; a sea lake; lads feed seals;

3. add leeks; she had leeks; he has a hall;

B.   Practise G key—F finger

Practise F to G
back to F. Keep
other fingers on
home keys

4. fff ggg fgf fgf fag fgf lag fgf sag fgf;

5. fgf jag fgf gag fgf hag fgf keg fgf leg;

C.   Practise U key—J finger

Practise J to U
back to J. Keep
little fingers on
home keys

6. jjj uuu juj juj due juj sue juj hue juj;

7. juj sug juj jug juj dug juj hug juj lug;

D.   Practise word-building

8. uuu sss eee ddd use uses used useful us;

9. jjj uuu ddd ggg eee judge judges judged;

E.   Apply the keys you know

10. he had a dull glass; a judge has a flag;   Feet firmly on floor

11. see she has a full jug; she used jaffas;

12. dad had a full keg; he shall guess; use;

Type a copy of the following on A4 paper. Use suitable margins and type in single spacing. Use figures for all numbers except at the beginning of a sentence or the figure one on its own.

APPLICATION FOR } All on one line please.
UNITED KINGDOM PASSPORT

Applicants under the age of 16 yrs. should complete Form "B" and those sixteen & over shd complete FORM "A". The present fee for a 10-year passport is £6.

The following important points shd be noted:

(a) A family passport is available to a wife & husband, & children under the age of 16.

(b) Applicants over 16 & under eighteen years of age shd hv the consent of a parent (or guardian) who must sign the Application Form "A".

v.c (c) All application forms must be countersigned by a British subject who has known the applicant(s) personally for at least two years & who is a Member of Parliament, Justice of the Peace, or person of similar standing.

v.c (d) 2 photographs of yourself must be enclosed w the application
v.c form. The photographs shd not be larger than 63 mm x 50 mm &
stet v.c the person countersigning yr. application form in (d) below above
shd endorse the reverse side of the photograph with the words [I
certify that this is a true likeness of Mr. (Mrs. or Miss) ... [& add
his/her signature.

Display the following on paper of suitable size.

AUCTION SALE [spaced caps

at the

Closed caps → Morecambe Hotel]
North Promenade] Single
BLACKPOOL] spacing

on

Thurs, 19th June, at 7.00 p.m.

v.c. Over 200 oil and watercolour paintings
Large collection of:

Please type [3 Jewellery (Diamond, Emerald / Sapphire)
in order
indicated. [4 Precious Stone Rings
Do not [2 Ladies / & Gentlemen's Watches
type
numbers. 5 Silverplate
1 Glass Tableware

Closed caps → Many unusual & interesting objets d'art

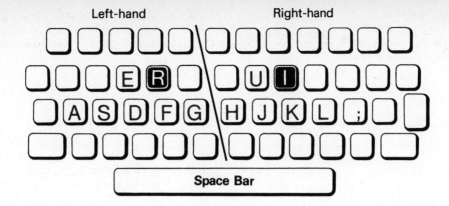

Left-hand   Right-hand

Space Bar

Type each line or sentence three times, saying the letters to yourself. If time permits, complete your practice by typing each group of lines as it appears. Keep your eyes on the copy and return the carriage sharply. Set left margin stop at 30 Elite, 22 Pica.

A. Review the keys you know

1. fds jkl ded juj fgf jhj hag jug dug leg;   Eyes on copy always
2. a lass uses a flask; all lads had a jug;
3. sell us a full keg; see she has a glass;

B. Practise R key—F finger

Practise F to R back to F. Keep other fingers on home keys

4. fff rrr frf frf jar frf far frf rag frf;
5. frf are frf ark frf red frf fur frf rug;

C. Practise I key—K finger

Practise K to I back to K. Keep other fingers on home keys

6. kkk iii kik kik kid kik lid kik did kik;
7. kik dig kik fig kik rig kik jig kik gig;

D. Practise word families

8. fill hill rill drill grill skill frills;
9. ark lark dark hark; air fair hair lairs;

E. Apply the keys you know

10. she likes a fair judge; he has dark hair   Sharp, brisk strokes
11. his lad fills a jug; she has rare skills
12. she is sure; ask her here; he likes figs

UNIT 5

Type the following exercise on a sheet of A5 landscape paper. Use block or centred style and rule.

THE CHRONICLE

ADVERTISING RATES

Classification	Per line	Semi-display per centimetre column	Full display per centimetre column
Charities) Jumble Sales)	£0.40	£1.75	£3.00
Church Announcements	£0.50	£2.00	£3.50
Property Exchanges) Employment Wanted) Private Messages)	£0.60	£3.--	£4.75
Theatres and Cinemas	£0.75	£3.10	£4.90
Public Announcements) Legal Notices) Tenders and Contracts)	£1.20	£6.30	£8.25 .

Type the following on headed memo form, taking a carbon copy.

To: Mr. A.S. Allsop (Scottish Office)　　Suitable Date

From: Lynne Barker (Head Office)

Subject: Conference & Annual Dinner

MALMESBURY

As requested in yr letter dated 4th Jan, I hv booked accommodation for you & Mrs. Allsop at the Royal Hotel, Malmesbury Park, Bournemouth, where, as you know, our Conference is being held.

N.P
U.c　As the journey may prove difficult by car at this time of year, our chairman suggests th you travel by night train fr Waverley Station on Sun., 6th Feb. You should book sleepers on this train.

As soon as poss. after the Conference, please send me a note of yr exs.

Left-hand   Right-hand

Space Bar

Type each line or sentence three times, saying the letters to yourself. If time permits, complete your practice by typing each group of lines as it appears. Keep your eyes on the copy and return the carriage sharply. Set left margin stop at 30 Elite, 22 Pica.

A. Review the keys you know

1. fgf jhj frf juj ded kik aid did her rug;
2. his full fees; she likes a dark red rug;
3. his girl is here; he is glad she is sure

Practise F to T back to F. Keep other fingers on home keys

B. Practise T key—F finger

4. fff ttt ftf ftf fit ftf kit ftf lit ftf;   Check your posture
5. ftf sit ftf hit ftf sat ftf hat ftf fat;

Practise L to O back to L. Keep other fingers on home keys

C. Practise O key—L finger

6. lll ooo lol lol lot lol got lol hot lol;
7. lol rot lol dot lol jot lol tot lol sot;

D. Practise word families

8. old hold sold gold; look rook hook took;
9. let set jet get ret; rate late hate date

E. Apply the keys you know

Back straight

10. get her a set; he took a full jar to her
11. he had sold the gold; at this late date;
12. that old dress looks just right for her;

Job 45   Production Target—ten minutes

The aim of this test is to see how much of the following exercise you type in ten minutes with not more than five errors.

Use double-line spacing and margins Elite 12–90, Pica 10–75. Erasers or other means of rectifying mistakes must NOT be used.

Office equipment and machinery can cost a great deal of money—	12
£600 would just cover the typist's basic needs, such as desk, chair,	26
typewriter and filing cabinet. If you have an electric typewriter	40
that alone will have cost your employer £250; or, if it is an electric	54
with proportional spacing, then £400 would be nearer the price.	66
Your employer, therefore, expects you to look after the machinery	79
and equipment that you use. He also expects the typist not to waste	93
paper, carbon paper, etc., because these are also expensive. Office	106
supplies used—and wasted—amount to huge sums of money over a	119
year, and your contribution towards economy is essential.	131
Work that is badly done is a sheer waste of time and money. For	149
example, a letter with finger marks on it, or carelessly corrected	157
errors will, if sent out, undermine a customer's confidence in your	170
Company. Perhaps you will type columns of figures and put in the	183
total without checking it. The total is wrong. Whose fault is it?	196
It is yours.	199
Before starting to type always read through the manuscript, or	211
whatever it may be, to see that you understand what you are about to	225
type. If you are in doubt about the meaning of a phrase or cannot	238
read the writing, ask the writer to clarify it for you. If you are	251
not sure about the spelling of a word, look in a dictionary.	263
If there are any general or specific instructions, amend the	275
passage clearly so that when you reach the point where the amend-	288
ment becomes effective, you will know what action to take.	300

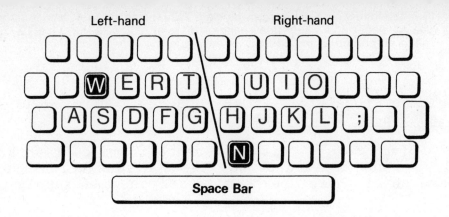

Type each line or sentence three times, saying the letters to yourself. If time permits, complete your practice by typing each group of lines as it appears. Keep your eyes on the copy and return the carriage sharply. Set left margin stop at 30 Elite, 22 Pica.

A. Review the keys you know

1. ftf lol frf juj ded kik tot out rot dot;

2. this is a red jet; the lad took the gold

3. he asked a just fee; the old folk agree;

Return carriage sharply without looking up

Practise S to W back to S. Keep F finger on home key

B. Practise W key—S finger

4. sss www sws sws low sws sow sws row sws;

5. sws hew sws few sws dew sws sew sws tew;

Practise J to N back to J. Keep little finger on home key

C. Practise N key—J finger

6. jjj nnn jnj jnj fan jnj ran jnj tan jnj;

7. jnj sin jnj kin jnj din jnj lin jnj tin;

D. Practise word families

8. end send lend tend fend rend wend trend;

9. low sow how row tow saw law daw jaw raw;

E. Apply the keys you know

10. we saw her look at the new gate; we knew

11. he sent us a gift of red jeans last week

12. we had left a jade silk gown and the rug

Wrist and arms straight, fingers curved

5. Type the following letter in semi-blocked style, using standard punctuation. Use A4 paper and single-line spacing. Margins: Elite 22–82, Pica 12–72. Take a carbon copy and address an envelope.

Your Ref. AB   Insert suitable date

Anglia Furniture Store Ltd., 250 High Street, Birmingham.   B23 2SN
For the attention of Mr. A. Burgess

Dear Sirs,   Divan Sets   With reference to my call on Friday last
(insert date) I have now decided to buy the 2 divans which I provisionally
selected, and shall therefore be glad if you will supply me with the
following:

      2 single Orange Seal Divan Sets,
        with orange cover, @ £36 each

      2 single Dralon Headboards,
        in oyster colour, @ £22 each

Enclosed is my cheque for £116 in settlement of this amount. [It was
arranged with Mr. A. Burgess that you would make delivery of the above
within the next 2 weeks, i.e., by the end of the month, and I hope you
will be able to do this.

Yours faithfully,   R. H. James

Record your progress   6½ minutes

R.31   Sunday is still a day of rest, but not to the extent   10
that it was years ago. In those days, because of the long   22
hours of work and bad working conditions in industry,   33
it was necessary for workers to be given a regular break in   45
order that the standard of their work should not suffer.   56
Sunday was the obvious day to choose, and regular attendance   68
at church, being a rest for both mind and body, was greatly   81
encouraged. Gardening, walking about or sitting in the park   92
or garden, was allowed, but any form of sport or strenuous   104
exercise was frowned upon, even to the extent of laws being   115
passed against them.   120

Now, however, with the shorter working week under good   130
working conditions for the most part, the need for absolute   142
relaxation of the body is not so vital. Even the housewife   154
has had much of the drudgery removed from her work by the   165
invention of labour-saving devices for her use, and she can   177
now more readily share the hobbies and the interests of the   189
rest of her family. How short is a shorter working week?   200
Prior to 1940, a 44-hour week was common-place for office   212
workers, and now they work a 35-hour week. (S.I. 1.40)   220

Set left margin stop at 30 Elite, 22 Pica

A.   Improve control of carriage return

1. Type the following lines exactly as shown. Repeat the exercise twice.

```
as a lass

as a lass falls

as a lass falls dad falls
```

Return carriage
sharply without
looking up

In the following exercises type each line three times, saying the letters to yourself.

B.   Improve control of [T] and [H] keys

```
2. the then than that this thus these there

3. she thus feels that this is rather good;

4. these lads are there for the third week;
```

C.   Improve control of space bar

Use right thumb and
even stroke

```
5. a s d f j k l ; g h w e r t u i o a s d;

6. at it we he go to as are not for did ask

7. we are sure he did not ask us for these;
```

D.   Improve control of [R] and [O] keys

```
8. our for road work word offer order other

9. she works near our road; the other word;

10. he wrote the order; sort out our offers;
```

E.   Improve control of paper insertion

By means of the paper release, take out the sheet of paper you are using. Put it back quickly in the machine, so that the left edge is at 0 on the carriage-position scale, and see that the paper is straight. Repeat this drill several times daily.

Displayed matter in semi-blocked letters

The usual method for displaying matter in semi-blocked letters is to arrange for the longest line to be centred in the typing line. To do this, find the centre point of the body of the letter by adding together the points at which the left and right margins are set and divide by two. Bring writing point to this scale-point and back-space once for every two letters and spaces in the longest line of the displayed matter. Always leave one clear space above and below displayed matter.

Practise semi-blocked letter with displayed matter

4. Type the following letter on A4 paper in semi-blocked style. Use standard punctuation and take a carbon copy. Margins: Elite 22–82, Pica 12–72.

Ref. LAB/PAC   23rd August, 1977

Atlas Wire Works Ltd.,
Farnborough Road,
Clifton,
NOTTINGHAM.
NG11 9AE

For the attention of Mr. H. W. Walker

Dear Sirs,

                            Crimped Wire

        We refer to your letter of the 24th June, 1977, enclos-
ing samples of nickel silver, phosphor bronze and brass wire.
We have now tested the samples sent and find this material
quite suitable for our manufactures.
                    (Turn up 2 single-line spaces)
        Before passing you our trial order, we shall be glad if
you will submit us a quotation for the following quantities,
bearing in mind that we use minimum monthly quantities of
200 kg of each type:
                    (Turn up 2 single-line spaces)
        25 kg Crimped Brass Wire, nickel silver, 0.12 mm
        25 kg Phosphor Bronze Wire, 0.20 mm
        25 kg Brass Wire, 0.15 mm
                    (Turn up 2 single-line spaces)
To be supplied on reels or coiled.

        In your quotation please state the shortest delivery
period and your terms of payment.

                        Yours faithfully,
                        H. WILKINS AND COMPANY

                        L. A. Butler
                        Buying Department.

Further exercise on displayed matter in semi-blocked letters is given on page 17 of **Practical Typing Exercises, Book One**

F.   Improve control of E and N keys

11. en end ten new knew then when need near;

12. then she went; he knew the news was sent   Feet firmly on floor

13. we need ten new jugs; near here; the end

G.   Improve control of W and I keys

14. win wish wife with will wait writ while;

15. his wife will wait with us; the wise lad

16. we will wish to write while we are there

H.   Improve control of U key

17. our hour four dull lull full hull gulls;

18. all our dull hours; four full weeks ago;

19. use our usual rules; let us rush out now

I.   Improve control of G key

20. go got good goods sigh sight light right

21. urge her to get a rug; the girl is right

22. go on the green light; the night is long

J.   Improve control of suffix ING

23. ing going taking selling dealing heating

24. he is going; we are selling; owing to us

25. ask if she is dealing with that heating;

K.   Apply the keys you know

26. now that joke is not good; our old safe;   Shoulders back and
relaxed

27. for fun ask if the jars she got were old

28. do join us; walk to that green fir tree;

UNIT 8

In a semi-blocked letter, turn up two single-line spaces after salutation and centre the heading over the body of the letter. To do this:
(a) Add together the points at which the left and right margins are set and divide by two.
(b) Bring the writing point to this scale-point and back-space once for every two letters and spaces in the subject heading.
(c) Type heading and underscore.
(d) Turn up two single-line spaces before starting the body of letter.

Practise typing semi-blocked letter with subject heading

3. Type the following letter on A5 portrait paper in semi-blocked style. Use standard punctuation. Margins: Elite 15–60, Pica 10–55.

```
Our Ref. HWW/ACF                    24th June, 1977

Messrs. H. Wilkins & Co.,
Cradock Road,
SHEFFIELD.
S2 21E

For the attention of Mr. L. A. Butler

Dear Sirs,
            (Turn up 2 single-line spaces)
                    Crimped Wire
            (Turn up 2 single-line spaces)
    As requested in your letter of the 22nd June,
we have pleasure in enclosing small samples of our
crimped wire in nickel silver, phosphor bronze and
brass.  This material can be supplied in any dimen-
sions to suit your requirements.

    We look forward to receiving a trial order
from you when you are in need of further supplies,
and shall be pleased to submit a quotation for
your requirements.

                    Yours faithfully,
                    ATLAS WIRE WORKS LTD.



                    H. W. Walker
                    Sales Manager

Enc.
```

Further exercises on semi-blocked letters with subject heading and standard punctuation are given on pages 14 and 15 of **Practical Typing Exercises, Book One**

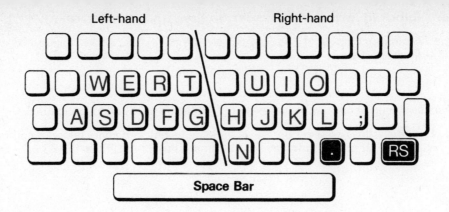

Space Bar

Type each line or sentence three times, saying the letters to yourself. If time permits, complete your practice by typing each group of lines as it appears. Keep your eyes on the copy and return the carriage sharply. Set left margin stop at 30 Elite, 22 Pica.

A.   Review the keys you know

1. sws jnj ftf lol frf jhj won win new now;   Eyes on copy

2. we do not like those jars she got for us

3. the red dogs will go for a walk just now

B.   Practise right shift key

To make capitals for letters typed by the left hand:
(a) With right hand little finger depress and hold right shift key well down.
(b) Strike left hand capital letter.
(c) Remove finger from shift key and return all fingers to home keys.

4. fF; dD; sS; aA; Ada; Sad; Dad; Fad; Wade

5. Gee; Reg; Ted; Sue; Flo; Ede; Dora; West

Practise L to . back
to L. Keep first
finger on home key

C.   Practise full stop key—L finger

6. lll ... l.l f.l j.l Good. Dear. Ellis.

TWO spaces after full stop at end of sentence

7. Ask her. Ted is sad. Do go. She will.

D.   Practise word families

8. Wee; Weed; Feed; Reed; Seed; Deed; Greed

9. And; Sand; Wand; Rand; Send; Tend; Fend;

E.   Apply the keys you know   Check your posture

10. Ask Ed Reid if we should join the Swede.

11. She was right. Dirk was jealous. Fine.

12. Flora would like to go; just state when.

Semi-blocked letter with 'attention line' and 'enclosure'

The 'Attention Line' and 'Enclosure' are typed in the same position as in fully-blocked letters.

Practise typing semi-blocked letter with 'Attention Line' and 'Enclosure'

2. Type the following letter on A4 paper in semi-blocked style, taking a carbon copy. Use standard punctuation. Margins: Elite 22–82, Pica 12–72.

Our Ref. LAB/PAC   22nd June, 1977

Atlas Wire Works Ltd.,
Farnborough Road,
Clifton,
NOTTINGHAM.
NG11 9AE
    (Turn up 2 single-line spaces)
For the attention of Mr. H. W. Walker
    (Turn up 2 single-line spaces)
Dear Sirs,

    We thank you for your letter of the 20th June, 1977, and note your remarks with regard to your manufactures.

    We regret to inform you that we ourselves do not make tooth-brushes. On the other hand, as you will see from the brochure enclosed, we do make brushes of all other kinds, and, although we have at the moment a sufficient stock to cover our requirements for the next 2 months, we should like to receive in the meantime a small sample showing the quality of your products.

    As soon as we are in need of further supplies of any of the material we use, we shall not fail to give you an opportunity of quoting us.

                Yours faithfully,
                H. WILKINS & CO.

                L. A. Butler
                Buying Department

Enc.

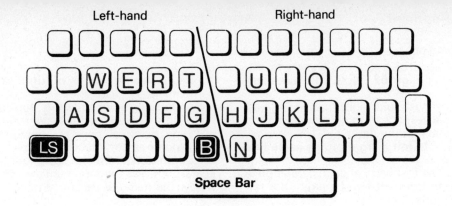

Space Bar

Type each line or sentence three times, saying the letters to yourself. If time permits, complete your practice by typing each group of lines as it appears. Keep your eyes on the copy and return the carriage sharply. Set left margin stop at 30 Elite, 22 Pica.

A. Review the keys you know

1. aA; sS; dD; fF; wW; eE; rR; Red; Gee; As

2. Ask Flo. See Roger. Tell Fred. Go in.

Two spaces after full stop at end of sentence

3. Ede had gone. Write to us. A fake jug.

B. Practise left shift key

To make capitals for letters typed by the right hand:
(a) With left hand little finger depress and hold left shift key well down.
(b) Strike right hand capital letter.
(c) Remove finger from shift key and return all fingers to home keys.

4. jJa kKa lLa jUj kIk Judd Kidd Lode Hoad;

Eyes on copy

5. Ida Ken Len Jude Owen Hilda Oakes Usual;

Practise F to B back to F. Keep little finger on home key

C. Practise B key—F finger

6. fff bbb fbf fbf bud fbf bus fbf but fbf;

7. fbf rob fbf sob fbf fob fbf hob fbf job;

D. Practise word families

8. Nib Jib Lib Job Lob Hob Hail Jail Nails;

9. Jill Hill Kill Lill Tall Ball Fall Wall;

E. Apply the keys you know

10. She will be taking those salads to Jane.

11. Jill knows. Kit had to bluff Bob Green.

12. Fred will ask us to do those jobs again.

Semi-blocked letter

The semi-blocked style of a letter is shown in the illustration given on page 62. Note the following points.

(a) *Date.* This ends flush with right margin. To find the starting point back-space from right margin once for each letter or space in the date.

(b) *Reference.* Type at left margin on the same line as the date.

(c) *Body of letter.* The first word of each paragraph is indented five spaces from left-hand margin. Set tab stop for paragraph indent.

(d) *Complimentary close.* Start this approximately at the centre of the typing line.

(e) *Signature*

 i. Begin typing name of firm at same point as complimentary close.

 ii. As in fully-blocked letters, turn up a minimum of five single-line spaces to leave room for signature.

iii. Type name of person signing, starting at same scale-point as complimentary close.

iv. Begin to type official designation (if any) at same scale-point as complimentary close immediately below the name of person signing.

The notes concerning open punctuation and forms of address given on page 77 apply also to semi-blocked letters.

Practise typing semi-blocked letter

1. Type the following semi-blocked letter, using A5 portrait paper. Set margins of Elite 15–60, Pica 10–55. Use standard punctuation.

```
Our ref. HWW/ACF                    20th June, 1977
     (Turn up 3 single-line spaces)


Messrs. H. Wilkins & Co.,
Cradock Road,
SHEFFIELD.
S2 21X
     (Turn up 3 single-line spaces)

Dear Sirs,

     We are suppliers of metal strip suitable
for the manufacture of tooth-brushes and other
types of brush, and are in a position to quote
you competitive prices and short delivery
periods.

     We can also supply wire in brass, nickel
silver and phosphor bronze, and if you are in
the market for such wire, we shall be pleased
to quote for your requirements.

     We look forward to hearing from you in
the near future.

                    Yours faithfully,
                    ATLAS WIRE WORKS LTD.


                    H. W. Walker
                    Sales Manager
```

A further exercise on semi-blocked letter is given on page 13 of **Practical Typing Exercises, Book One**

Left-hand | Right-hand

Space Bar

Type each line or sentence three times, saying the letters to yourself. If time permits, complete your practice by typing each group of lines as it appears. Keep your eyes on the copy and return the carriage sharply. Set left margin stop at 25 Elite, 18 Pica.

A. Review the keys you know

1. fbf sws jnj ftf lol frf jhj Len Ken Hen Ian Win Go

Two spaces after full stop at end of sentence

2. Dan and Rob left. He will go just now. Ask Nell.

3. Lois and Earl will see June. Go with Fred Bolton.

Practise J to M back to J. Keep little finger on home key

B. Practise M Key—J finger

4. jjj mmm jmj jmj jam jmj ham jmj dam jmj ram jmjmj;

5. jmj rum jmj hum jmj sum jmj mum jmj gum jmj strum;

C. Practise left and right shift keys

6. Ada Ben Dan East Fred Green Hilda Irwin James King

7. Lil Mark Nell Owen Rene Sara Todd Usher Wills Watt

Little fingers for shift keys

D. Practise word families

8. arm farm harm warm alarm art hart tart darts mart;

9. game name dame fame same lame home dome some foam;

E. Apply the keys you know

10. Most of the fame goes to John who had been working hard for his father but he has now left the works. I think he is now at home.

Skill building

Type each exercise (A and B) three times. Keep your eyes on the copy and return the carriage sharply.

Margins:
Elite 22–82
Pica 12–72

A.   Review alphabet keys

1.   You must emphasise the importance of that exceptionally quaint jewellery which is being removed from the bank today.

B.   Build accuracy on suffix drill

2. action station mention question decision education exception

3. liable payable capable notable suitable advisable honourable

4. Is she capable of making an honourable decision on the question of education? She may mention many notable exceptions.

Accuracy practice   30 w.p.m.   6½ minutes   Not more than four errors

For this exercise change margins to Elite 18–90, Pica 10–75

A.57 How exciting it would be if, suddenly, all employers in this	12
country gave employees a rise of £30 a week. Can you visualise all	25
the things you could do—buy new clothes, a new car, holidays in	38
the Bahamas? However, your elation would be short-lived because	51
such a grand-scale pay rise would mean only one thing—inflation.	64
Economists tell us that we have inflation when there is too	76
much money chasing too few goods. In other words, unless our total	89
production of goods and services—the gross national product—	102
increases, nobody is better off. With a pay increase of £30 a week	115
for all employees, cars, holidays, etc., would all rise in price in	128
a similar proportion.	133
When our prices rise, it means that other countries will not	145
buy our products, and this would lead to a deficit in our Balance	158
of Payments. Also, when prices rise, people who live on fixed	170
incomes (pensioners, for instance) do not always get increases,	182
and, therefore, they would be at a much greater disadvantage.	195

(S.I. 1.40)

Speed building   45 w.p.m.   Two minutes   Not more than four errors

S.16 It is with much regret that I have to tell you that our	11
Chairman, Mr. Birch, has decided to retire from the Board of	23
Directors at the end of this year. We shall all miss him	34
very much, and we wish to express our sincere gratitude for	46
the very fine work he has done for the firm during the past	58
30 years. I feel sure that all of you here today would like	70
to join with me in wishing him long years of good health and	82
happiness in his well-earned retirement. (S.I. 1.22)	90

1 | 2 | 3 | 4 | 5 | 6 | 7 | 8 | 9 | 10 | 11 | 12 |

UNIT 93   152

Improvement Practice

Type each line or sentence three times, saying the letters to yourself. If time permits, complete your practice by typing each group of lines as it appears. Keep your eyes on the copy and return the carriage sharply. Set left margin stop at 25 Elite, 18 Pica.

A.   Improve control of home row keys

Two spaces after full stop at the end of sentence

1. add had jag gas ask ash sash dash glad flags flash

2. Dad has a flag.   Sal had a sash.   A lass asks dad.

3. A lass had had a jag.   A glad lad.   Ask a sad lad.

B.   Improve control of O and U keys

4. to go now out our hour tour sour would house shout

5. Ask Ruth if she would like to go to our house now.

6. Tell Flo we will start out on our tour in an hour.

C.   Improve control of carriage return

7. I will go
   I will go soon
   I will go as soon as
   I will go as soon as I get there.

D.   Improve control of W E R and T keys

8. we wet were west tree tell test three threw refers

9. We three were there.   I saw those trees last week.

10. She referred to the tests.   Tell her to rest here.

E.   Improve control of shift keys

11. He Ask Jon Sara Kite Dale Lord Ford Hall Iris Tait

12. Ask Mrs. Ford if she will see Mr. Tait in an hour.

ONE space only after full stop in Mr. and Mrs.

13. Owen Dale and Gerald Reid are going to Harrow now.

Review Quiz No. 7

1. Postcards need not have a ... or a ... ...
2. When an item takes more than one line, leader dots are typed on the ... line of the item.
3. Groups of leader dots must be typed ... one another in all lines.
4. Leader dots must ... be typed right up to the preceding or following ...
5. ... word or letter must extend beyond the last leader dot on the line.
6. When typing subdivided columns in a table, type the ... column heading first.
7. In figure columns the longest item is centred and other figures typed so that ... are under units, ... under tens, etc.
8. In circular letters the names and addresses may be ... or ... left for these.
9. The words 'Date as postmark' are often typed instead of the date in the ... position of the date.
10. When typing a letter with 'tear-off' this should end about ... ... from bottom of page.
11. Type ... ... or ... from edge to edge of paper for a 'tear-off' form.
12. When filling in details on form letters, etc., leave ... clear space after last character.
13. In tabulation always ... each horizontal line before starting the next.
14. In open punctuation ... full stop must be used ... abbreviations.
15. Small Roman numerals are used for ... or ...
16. Words should not be divided on more than ... consecutive lines.
17. ... full stop after last word in a heading unless the word is ...

Check your answers below. Score one point for each correct entry.
Total score: 28

Answers
Review quizzes

No. 1 (page 46)
1. One 2. Two 3. Two 4. No 5. Five 6. No 7. No, Two 8. Cover 9. One 10. Flat, Straight, Straight 11. 82, 100 12. 70, 35, 50. 13. No 14. Not 15. Shift 16. One 17. No 18. A4, A5 portrait, A5 landscape 19. Shift lock 20. Hyphen 21. Not, Two 22. Not 23. Not, Two 24. Abbreviations, Proper. 25. Not

No. 2 (page 60)
1. Same point 2. Single, Double, Five, Left 3. Three 4. Two, Right 5. Centre, Blocked 6. One, Three 7. No, One 8. Blocked, Centred, One 9. Three 10. Underscored 11. Blocked, Indented 12. Closed, Left, One. 13. Inside, Closed, Underscore. 14. Not 15. One, After, Before 16. x, Lower 17. Not 18. Not

No. 3 (page 81)
1. No, No 2. No, No 3. Not, p 4. Nought, Before 5. On 6. Six, One 7. Two, Before, One 8. Closed capitals 9. Four 10. Left Margin 11. Two 12. Postcode, Six, Right 13. No 14. Three 15. Closed Capitals 16. Enc, Encs, Left, Two 17. Left Margin 18. No 19. No, One 20. Courtesy, Not, Title

No. 4 (page 103)
1. Ampersand, Firms, Numbers 2. NP, [3. Inserted, Deleted 4. Tab stops, Margins 5. 0 6. Once, Two Characters, Spaces 7. Heading, Items 8. Left Margin, Tab Stop 9. Left Margin 10. Three 11. Spaces 12. Two, Fractions, Next 13. Three, Five, Width 14. Left Margin, Tab Stop 15. Margin Release, Two 16. Right Margin, One, Two 17. Full Stop, No 18. Comma, Last, No. 19. Comma, Space

No. 5 (page 121)
1. Two 2. Unit 3. Interliner 4. Return, Interliner 5. Above, Below 6. Vertical 7. Middle 8. Bottom 9. Above, Below 10. Vertical lines 11. Three, Five 12. Memorandum 13. Left, Platen Roller 14. Variable Line-Spacer 15. Above, Below 16. Salutation, Complimentary Close 17. Two clear 18. Enc, Encs, Left 19. Above, Alignment Scale 20. Courtesy Title 21. Right, Left Margin

No. 6 (page 137)
1. Seller, Buyer 2. VAT 3. Credit Note 4. Summary 5. u.c., l.c. 6. Continuous Brackets 7. Solidus, Underscore 8. x, hyphen 9. Capital I, small l 10. Below 11. Above 12. Two 13. No, One 14. No, 15. One, Before, One 16. Consistent 17. No

No. 7 (page 151)
1. Salutation, Complimentary Close 2. Second 3. Underneath 4. Not, Character 5. No 6. Deepest 7. Units, Tens 8. Omitted, Space 9. Normal 10. One inch 11. Continuous Hyphens, Dots 12. One 13. Complete 14. No, After 15. Prefaces, Sub-sections 16. Two 17. No, Abbreviated

Books of Reference (page 46)

1. Meaning and Spelling of Word 2. Correct postal address 3. To locate streets and roads 4. Synonyms and Antonyms 5. Correct telephone number 6. Check location of town 7. Useful typing hints

F. Improve control of I and N keys

14. an is in into line infer night noise injure inside
15. Irene infers Nina was injured one night this week.
16. The noise is inside the inn. Neither one will go.

G. Improve control when typing phrases

Brisk, even strokes

17. to go to us to see to ask to take to fill to write
18. I wish to see Wales. Ask her to fill in the date.
19. Leslie would like to take Jill to the new theatre.

H. Improve control of B key

20. bid but bad best both able book begin about better
21. Both of us will be better off when he begins work.
22. Bob has been able to book a table for Bill and me.

I. Improve control of M key

23. am me man seem make main must item them from might
24. I am making out a form for the main items we lost.
25. I must tell him that the amount seems to be right.

J. Improve control of space bar

Use right thumb and even strokes

26. a w s e d r f t g b h j n u m k i o l f b j n m l.
27. is it if in as an at am on or of to go he me we be
28. He did go to tea. It is now time for us to go on.

Type a copy of the following on A4 paper, using double spacing. The heading underscored in the body should be typed as a shoulder heading. Use indented paragraphs unless otherwise instructed.

DUPLICATING METHODS

1. Stencilling   *underscore*

A stencil consists of a sheet of tough, thin, fibrous paper base

lc wh is impregnated or coated with a wax|like composition.

NP [For convenience in handling it, the mfr fastens the stencil sheet to

a stiff backing sheet. The stencil may be cut by typewriter, /or it

may be cut by hand w a special pen.   *(in wh case the ribbon is disengaged,)*

C Preparatory Steps.   There are certain/ s⁀teps to take before ~~you~~ start*ing*

(preparatory)

to type a stencil.   These are as follows:-

1. See th the type-faces are thoroughly clean.   Clean the type|both *-faces*

trs   ⁀after and/ before cutting the stencil.

3 *2*.   Insert the stencil in the machine, making sure th the carbon &

as well as

backing sheet ~~and~~ the stencil itself li|e flat on the platen, as *oy*

otherwise creases or cracks can occur.

2 *3*.   Place the ribbon-switch in the /stencil/ position.   *"/ "/*

Typist: Use single spacing for numbered paras. + block at left margin

Record your progress   Six minutes

R.30   Epsom is known all over the world as the place   10
              where the great horse race, the Derby, is run each year, but it   21
              has also given its name to the well-known Epsom Salts.   32
                   The small village was not known outside the immediate   43
              district until early in the seventeenth century, and it is   55
              said that one day a herdsman, much to his joy, found on the   78
              common a water-hole which he did not know was there. He   89
              hoped to water his sheep there, but they refused to drink   100
              because the water was so bitter. This was at a time when it   112
              was a popular habit to drink spa waters for most human ail-   124
              ments. This water was soon recognised as a healing water,   136
              a great blood purifier, and named Epsom Water. Soon visitors   148
              flocked in from all over Europe, and it was not long before   160
              the craze for taking spa water was in full spate at Epsom as   172
              elsewhere. Fashions change, however, and as this craze died,   184
              helped no doubt by the coming on to the market of an artificial   196
              Epsom Salt, the spa at Epsom was no more.   (S.I. 1.30)   205

Check your work after each exercise

After returning the carriage sharply, check each exercise carefully.

1. Each incorrect spacing counts one error.	1. They haveto leave early.
2. Each incorrect punctuation counts one error.	2. They have to leave early,
3. Each 'raised' capital counts one error.	3. ᵀhey have to leave early.
4. Each wrong indentation or line-spacing counts one error.	4. They have to leave early.
5. Lightly struck letters count as one error.	5. They have to leave early.

One-minute goals

1. Type the exercise. If any word causes you to hesitate, type that word three times.
2. Take a one-minute timing.
3. If you reach the goal, or beyond, take another timing and see if you can type the same number of words but with fewer mistakes.
4. If you do not reach the goal after three tries, you need a little more practice on the key drills. Choose the previous exercise(s) that give intensive practice on the keys that caused difficulty.

Notes:
(a) There is little to be gained by typing any one drill more than three times consecutively. When you have typed it three times, go on to another drill; then, if necessary, go back to the original drill.

(b) At present, techniques (striking the keys evenly and sharply, good posture, eyes on copy, returning the carriage without looking up) are very important and you should concentrate on good techniques. If your techniques are right, then accuracy will follow. However, if you have more than two errors for each minute typed, it could mean that you have not practised the new keys sufficiently and that you should go back and do further intensive practice on certain key drills.

Measure your speed

You should be able to type to the 'tick-tock' rhythm of the clock. Bounce your fingers off the keys, one stroke for the 'tick' and one stroke for the 'tock'. Say the 'tick-tock' to yourself as you strike the keys. Remember to include the punctuation marks and space bar. If you have a record player, you can use the Gregg Typing Records to pace your striking of the keys.

Five strokes count as one 'standard' word. In a typing line of 50 spaces there are ten 'standard' words. The figures to the right of each exercise indicate the number of 'standard' words in the complete line, and the scale below indicates the number across the page. If in the exercise below you reach the word 'we' in one minute, your speed is $10 + 6 = 16$ words per minute. You will now be able to measure and record your speed.

Type the following exercise as instructed under Nos. 1–4 of 'One-Minute Goals'. Set left margin at 25 Elite, 18 Pica.

Goal—16 words in one minute

We will take her to see our new house on the north   10

side of the new estates and we¹⁶shall ask George to   20

join us at that time. **(S.I. 1.04)**   24

1 ‖ 2 ‖ 3 ‖ 4 ‖ 5 ‖ 6 ‖ 7 ‖ 8 ‖ 9 ‖ 10 ‖

Type the following on a sheet of A4 paper, using suitable margins. Follow the layout exactly.

<u>P A P E R　　S I Z E S</u>

The 3 main sizes of typing paper are:

A4 = $8\frac{1}{4}$" x $11\frac{3}{4}$" (210 x 297 mm)
A5 (landscape) = $8\frac{1}{4}$" x $5\frac{7}{8}$" (210 x 148 mm)
A5 (portrait) = $5\frac{7}{8}$" x $8\frac{1}{4}$" (148 x 210 mm)

<u>HORIZONTAL SPACING</u>

<u>Elite</u>

A4 = 100 - centre point 50　　　　　　　) 12 spaces
A5 (landscape) = 100 - centre point 50) =
A5 (portrait) = 70 - centre point 35　) 1" (25 mm)

<u>Pica</u>

A4 = 82 - centre point 41　　　　　　　) 10 spaces
A5 (landscape) = 82 - centre point 41) =
A5 (portrait) = 59 - centre point 29) 1" (25 mm)

<u>VERTICAL LINE SPACING</u>

A4 = 70 lines　　　　　　　) 6 lines
A5 (landscape) = 35 lines) =
A5 (portrait) = 50 lines) 1"

To leave $\frac{1}{2}$" clear, turn up　4 single-line spaces
"　"　1"　"　　"　"　7　"　"
"　"　$1\frac{1}{2}$"　"　　"　" 10　"　"
"　"　2"　"　　"　" 13　"　"
"　"　$2\frac{1}{2}$"　"　　"　" 16　"　"
"　"　3"　"　　"　" 19　"　"

Main headings are normally centred over the typing line.　To find centre point of typing line, add together the points at which the margins are set and divide total by 2, e.g., margins 20 and 85 = 105 ÷ 2 = 52 (centre point).

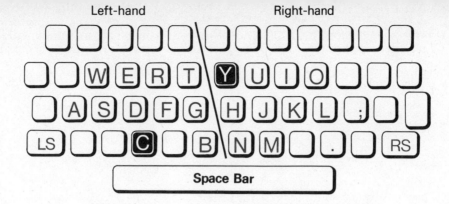

Left-hand   Right-hand

Type each line or sentence three times, saying the letters to yourself. If time permits, complete your practice by typing each group of lines as it appears. Keep your eyes on the copy and return the carriage sharply. Set left margin stop at 25 Elite, 18 Pica.

A. Review the keys you know

1. jmj fmj kmk fmf lml am; Mat Tom Ham Sam Lamb Farm;   Eyes on copy
2. Mr. Lamb would like to take on the job we offered.
3. None of them would go with Job down the long road.

Practise D to C back to D. Keep little finger on home key

B. Practise C key—D finger

4. ddd ccc dcd dcd cod dcd cot dcd cob dcd cog dcdcd;
5. dcd cut dcd cub dcd cur dcd cud dcd cab dcd cat cd

Practise J to Y back to J. Keep other fingers on home keys

C. Practise Y key—J finger

6. jjj yyy jyj jyj jay jyj hay jyj lay jyj bay jyjyj;
7. jyj say jyj day jyj ray jyj may jyj gay jyj way jj

D. Practise word families

8. sty try fry dry cry wry dice rice mice nice trice;   Brisk, even strokes
9. shy sky sly try sty slay stay fray gray dray stray

E. Apply the keys you know

Goal—16 words in one minute

10. He is not able to find a nice jacket which he says   10

     he lost on the way to your farm.[16] He will send you   20

     his bill in a week or so. (S.I. 1.08)   25

     1 | 2 | 3 | 4 | 5 | 6 | 7 | 8 | 9 | 10 |

UNIT 14   21

(a) Type the following circular letter on A4 paper. Use open or closed punctuation. Take a carbon copy. Reminder: Tear-off portion to be in double spacing.

Our ref. MG/JH
Date as postmark
(leave sufficient space for the name and address of
addressee to be inserted at a later date)

Dear Sir/Madam   SCOTTISH CUT GLASS

We are now offering delightful crystal glasses at most
reasonable prices. These glasses have the ring and
27 elegance which comes from a superb design which can only
give pleasure.

le.   Sherry Glasses   £7.35 each
      Dinner wine glasses   £8.27 "
      Champagne glasses   £10.83 "   (slender and
Trs/ Wine goblets   £8.74 "   fluted)
      Heavy tumblers   £8.92 "

We feel sure that you will want to know about these
exquisite glasses. If you would be kind enough to complete the tear-off portion at the foot of this letter and
send it to us, we shall be delighted to send you our
current catalogue.
Yours ffy.   THE SCOTTISH CUT GLASS CO. LTD. Morag Gillespie (Miss)
                                              Managing Director

- -

To: Morag Gillespie, Managing Director,
    The Scottish Cut Glass Co. Ltd., Bannockburn, Stirling.
                                            FK7 8LZ
Please send me your current catalogue of Scottish Cut Glass.
Surname (Mr./Mrs./Miss). . . . . _ . . . Initials . . . .
Address . . . .

- - - - - - - - - - - - - - - - Town . - - - - - - - -
County - - - - - - - - . Postcode - - - - - - -
Date - - - - - - - . Telephone Number - - - -

      Please complete the above in block letters

(b) On carbon copy fill in your name, address, etc.

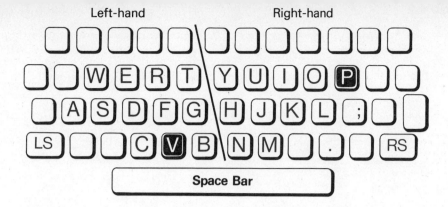

Type each line or sentence three times, saying the letters to yourself. If time permits, complete your practice by typing each group of lines as it appears. Keep your eyes on the copy and return the carriage sharply. Set left margin stop at 25 Elite, 18 Pica.

A. Review the keys you know

1. dcd jyj dcd fbf jhj fgf lol yet coy yes call come.   Eyes on copy
2. Her mother had brought a new kind of jersey cloth.
3. He sent us a ticket for the jumble sale on Monday.

B. Practise P key—; finger

Practise ; to P back to ; Keep J finger on home key and other fingers curved

4. ;;; ppp ;p; ;p; cap ;p; lap ;p; rap ;p; jap p;p;p;
5. ;p; pip ;p; dip ;p; sip ;p; hip ;p; lip ;p; nip p;

C. Practise V key—F finger

Practise F to V back to F. Keep little finger on home key

6. fff vvv fvf fvf vow fvf van fvf vat fvf vet fvfvf;
7. fvf eve fvf vie fvf via fvf very fvf give fvf five

D. Practise word families

8. tup cup pup sup lop pop fop hop cop top tops mops;
9. live five hive dive give rave pave save wave gave;

E. Apply the keys you know

Goal—17 words in one minute

10. She moved a pink jug away from the very back shelf   10

     where it had been hidden from sight.[17] It now shows   20

     up better on that top shelf. (S.I. 1.15)   26

    1 | 2 | 3 | 4 | 5 | 6 | 7 | 8 | 9 | 10 |

UNIT 15   **22**

Type the following on a memo form. Use suitable date. The memo is from 'Carmel Barnes' to 'Peter Thacker' and the subject heading is SALARY SETTLEMENT—JUNE 1977. Take two carbon copies. On the first carbon copy type in the top left-hand corner—Miss M. H. Gill—for information.

u.c./
figs./
27

ch

Certain difficulties have arisen in the translation of the recent award given to secretarial grades. As it is your wish that the (two) months' back pay should be paid at the end of this month, I confirm our telephone conversation with you when it was agreed that we have a meeting with Miss M. H. Gill on Monday next (please insert date) to discuss the points raised on the attached sheet.

Type the following letter on A4 paper. Use today's date. The sender's address is: 209 Bradford Street, Leeds LS4 5SP. To: Union Insurance Co. Ltd., Calvery Street, Leeds LS1 3AE For the attention of the Manager—Claims Department. Heading: Policy No. 1789

Insert Ref. FSS/IES

Dear Sirs   I regret to inform you that a burglary occurred last night at the above address.
The house was occupied at the time by myself and my family, and the burglars forced an entrance through the kitchen door. We were not disturbed so that we have been unable to assist the local police who have been investigating the matter. However, I would state that all possible precautions have been taken to safeguard my property, and the loss incurred was not due to carelessness or negligence on my part. On the attached list I give details of the missing property, and shall be glad to receive a copy of your official Claim Form.
Yrs. ffy F. S. Somers

27

always/

NP/
lc/

#

On suitable paper type the following credit note No. D8754 from The Universal Supply Co. Ltd., 84–114 High Street, Aberdeen. AB2 3HE. VAT Reg. No. 992 3872 78. Dated 15th July, 1977. To: M. S. Carmichael & Co. Ltd., Leith Walk, Edinburgh. EH6 8NY.

Reason for credit: Damaged goods
Quantity and description: 1 64-Watt Stereo Amplifer £100.
VAT: Rate 25%—Amount £25.
Total Credit: £100. Total VAT: £25. Total amount credited: £125.
Original tax invoice No. 1984 dated 24th June, 1977.

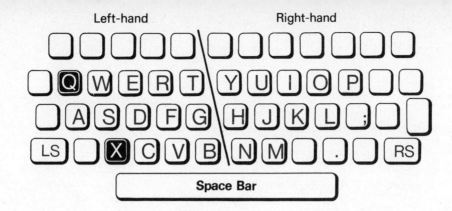

Space Bar

Type each line or sentence three times, saying the letters to yourself. If time permits, complete your practice by typing each group of lines as it appears. Keep your eyes on the copy and return the carriage sharply. Set left margin stop at 25 Elite, 18 Pica.

A.   Review the keys you know

1. ;p; fvf ftf jhj dpf apf kpf pot van cop map eve p;   Fingers curved
2. Jack was glad my family all moved to North Avenue.
3. Daniel may have to give back a few paper journals.

Practise S to X back to S. Keep first finger on home key

B.   Practise X key—S finger

4. sss xxx sxs sxs tax sxs lax sxs pax sxs wax sxsxs;
5. sxs sex sxs hex sxs vex sxs rex sxs cox sxs vox xs

Practise A to Q back to A. Keep first finger on home key

C.   Practise Q key—A finger

6. aaa qqq aqa aqa quad aqa aqua aqa equal aqa quick;
7. aqa quin aqa quit aqa quite aqa equal aqa query qa

D.   Practise word families

8. qua quad squad quit quip quins quill quint quilts;
9. fox cox mix six fix nix axe pax wax tax taxi taxed

E.   Apply the keys you know

Goal—17 words in one minute

10. Joe quickly moved the gross of new boxes for which   10

    you had paid and then took an extra[17]box of the red   20

    quilts and sheets you wanted. (S.I. 1.15)   26

    1 | 2 | 3 | 4 | 5 | 6 | 7 | 8 | 9 | 10 |

Production typing

Job 37   Production Target—eight minutes

Display the following Menu on A5 portrait paper. Follow instructions carefully.

J. HEATH & CO. LTD.

ANNUAL DINNER   ] *Spaced caps*   *Typist—please centre all lines*

MENU

Salmon Mousse in Aspic

Mushroom Soup

Roast Saddle of Lamb

Redcurrant Jelly   ] *Single spacing*

trs.   *Cauliflower w. Cheese Sauce*

Roast Potatoes

Cold Lemon Meringue

Coffee

Job 38   Production Target—twenty minutes

Display the following boxed table with closed sides on A4 paper in double spacing. Insert leader dots and use block or centred style. Type in order indicated but omit numbers.

Budget for the year ended 31st December, 1976

		Nett exclusive of VAT	VAT	Total inclusive of VAT	
	-----	£	£	£	
3	Meeting expenses ..	204.94	16.39	221.33	
6	Telephone and Telex ..	3 149.63	11.17	150.80	trs
5	Printing and Stationery	147.69	11.81	159.80	5
2	Insurance	5.50	Exempt	5.50	
1	Annual Outing	247.00	19.76	266.86	7
4	Postages	194.14	Exempt	194.14	
7	Travelling Expenses Train Fares	194.00	Zero Rated	194.00	
		£1,132.90	£59.13	£1,192.03	

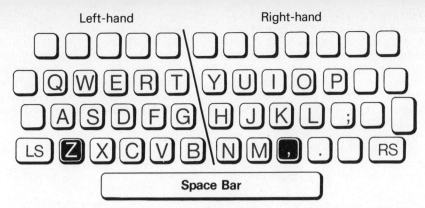

Left-hand   Right-hand

Space Bar

Type each line or sentence three times, saying the letters to yourself. If time permits, complete your practice by typing each group of lines as it appears. Keep your eyes on the copy and return the carriage sharply. Set left margin stop at 25 Elite, 18 Pica.

A. Review the keys you know

1. axs aqa fxf fcf axs xaj sex vex tax quit aqua quad
2. Just have one box of new grey mats packed quickly.
3. With extra help Clive found many quite black jugs.

Practise A to Z back to A. Keep first finger on home key

B. Practise Z key—A finger

4. aaa zzz aza aza zoo aza zinc aza zeal aza azure za
5. aza zip aza zero aza size aza gaze aza jazz aza za

Practise K to , back to K. Keep little finger on home key

C. Practise , key—K finger

6. kkk ,,, k,k k,k l,k a,k s,k j,k d,k f,k hj,k gf,k,

One space after comma

7. at, it, is, or, if, one, can, yes, may, for, cross

D. Practise word families

8. daze haze gaze laze maze, lazy hazy crazy, puzzle.
9. zeal zero zest zone, size prize, buzz fuzz, azure.

E. Apply the keys you know

Goal—18 words in one minute

10. We do hope the right size is in stock; yes, it is;   10

    we have just a few boxes, but the colour,[18] although   20

    quite pretty, is not the same. (S.I. 1.15)   26

Feet apart, firmly on floor

1 | 2 | 3 | 4 | 5 | 6 | 7 | 8 | 9 | 10 |

Sometimes a letter will have a tear-off portion at the foot so that a customer can fill in certain details and return the tear-off portion to the sender.

The typing on the tear-off section should end about an inch (25 mm) from the bottom of the page and any space not required for the tear-off portion should be left after the Complimentary Close or the name of the signatory if this is given.

The minimum space to be left after the Complimentary Close or signatory is four clear spaces. In other words, turn up a minimum of five single-line spaces and then type, from *edge to edge* of the paper *continuous dots* or *continuous hyphens*; then turn up two single-line spaces and type the information on the tear-off portion.

When blank spaces are left for details to be filled in, use *continuous dots* or the *underscore* and double spacing. Remember to leave one clear space after the last character typed before starting the dots or underscore and one clear space at the end of the dots or underscore before the next typed character if there is one, e.g.,

(space)   (space)   (space)

Surname .... Christian names ....

Practise typing letter with tear-off portion

2. Type the following letter on A4 paper in single-line spacing in block style. Leave sufficient space for name and address of addressee. Margins: Elite 18—83, Pica 10—75.

Our Ref PW/SM   Date as Postmark

Dear Sir

High Income Investment

In these days of inflation a high yield from your Capital is not enough; it is essential also to protect the real value of your capital. Our new Income Investment scheme has been designed to meet this requirement.

By investing in selected ordinary shares we aim not only to pro-vide an income which starts at a high level and which will go on growing, but also to provide the growth increase needed to keep the value of your investment in line with ahead of inflation. This is the advantage that our High Income investment has over other forms of investment which are not designed to combat inflation. If you require any further information, complete the form below and return it to us, when our representative will make an appointment to see you. suit your convenience.

Yours faithfully,
20th Century Investment Co Ltd

PETER WILLIAMSON
Director

Please send me full details of your High Income Investment Scheme.

SURNAME .... Christian Name(s) ....

ADDRESS ....

....

A further exercise on letter with tear-off portion is given on page 63 of **Practical Typing Exercises, Book One**

Improvement Practice

Type each line or sentence three times, saying the letters to yourself. If time permits, complete your practice by typing each group of lines as it appears. Keep your eyes on the copy and return the carriage sharply. Set left margin stop at 25 Elite, 18 Pica.

A.   Improve control of carriage return

1. Type the following lines exactly as shown.
   Repeat the exercise twice

```
It was good
It was good to see
It was good to see you
It was good to see you and her
It was good to see you and her today
```

Return carriage sharply without looking up

B.   Improve control of [B] and [M]

2. mob bump brim Mabel blame bloom climb bombs became
3. Blame Mabel.   The mob climbed in through a window.
4. My rose bloom became well known.   I bumped my car.

TWO spaces after . at end of sentence

C.   Improve control of punctuation

5. I shall tell Wilfred.   No, he may be rather angry.
6. We are pleased to hear from you; but we cannot go.
7. John, Mary and Elsie are going.   You may come too.

ONE space after ; and ,

D.   Improve control of [C] and [Y] keys

8. cry city clay copy cozy carry yacht comply certify
9. I certify that this is a copy; it is quite correct
10. Cathy must comply with the order.   The yacht left.

E.   Improve control of space bar

11. at it up on to we an be go of so am by do as no he
12. Go to her.   It is up to us.   I am here.   Tell him.
13. If you go to the shop now, he will still be there.

Use right thumb and even strokes

Our Ref. AB/JCB   Date as postmark

(Turn up 9 single-line spaces)

Dear Sir,

We are introducing a new PLASTIC WALL COATING for external use. Not only will this improve the appearance of the walls of your house, but it will also provide the walls with a plastic raincoat and insulate against the winter cold, eliminate dampness, and seal cracks and holes. Also, future maintenance will be avoided, as it has a minimum guaranteed life expectancy of 15 years.

The type of property which you own appears to be very suit-able for our new PLASTIC WALL COATING. If your house is suffering from any of the following problems:

1.   BRICKWORK - pointing in bad condition, bricks fibrous
      or porous;

2.   STUCCO AND PEBBLE DASH - cracked, sandy and soft, pebbles
      falling off;

3.   CEMENT RENDER - cracked, hollow patches, breaking away;

4.   DAMP IN THE WALLS - showing inside or out;

we can cure all or any of these defects and transform the appearance of your property by the application of this coat-ing - which will not only beautify and protect your house but will also increase its value.

If this offer appeals to you, please complete and post the enclosed card to us. All estimates are entirely free.

Yours faithfully,
PLASTICS PRODUCTS LTD.

A. Boggan (Miss)
Marketing Manager.

Enc.

F. Improve control of **P** and **V** keys

14. pave prove vapour provide private prevent provoked
15. I will provide a private plane. We will prove it.
16. Prevent Peter from provoking Val and Victor Payne.

G. Improve control of shift keys

17. Sal Joe Fay Ida Roy Lee Don Gay Bob Your Mary Hall
18. Tell Joe, Fay, Lee and Marie to call on Roy Young.
19. Edna Kelly and Nan Peters will visit Olive Walker.

Hold shift key well down with little finger

H. Improve control of **Q** and **X** keys

20. mix tax vex exit next taxi; quay quiz quite quiet;
21. A taxi will be at the quay exit; expect him there.
22. Keep quite quiet in that queue for this next quiz.

I. Improve control of phrases

23. to go, to ask, to see, to pay, to hear, to let him
24. I am pleased to hear that you are going to see me.
25. Remember to go and to ask her to pay for the flat.

J. Improve control of **Z** and **,**

26. zip, size, lazy, zeal, zone, prize, dozen, amazed,
27. I was amazed, quite amazed, to see a dozen prizes.
28. We gazed at the zebra, also a gazelle, in the zoo.

K. Apply the keys you know

Goal—18 words in one minute

29. The whizzing of a jet plane across the sky had now   10

    become such a normal event that it won[18]but a quick   20

    glance from the young boys in the crowd. (S.I. 1.14)   28

    1 | 2 | 3 | 4 | 5 | 6 | 7 | 8 | 9 | 10 |

Circular letters

Circulars or circular letters are letters (the contents of which are the same) which are sent to a number of customers or clients. The original is usually typed on a master sheet (stencil or offset litho) and a quantity is 'run off'.

Reference—in usual position

Date—typed in various ways; e.g., 21st July, 1977
July, 1977 (month and year only)

Follow instructions or layout — Date as postmark (these words are typed in the position where you normally type the date).

Name and address of addressee—

(a) Space may be left for this, and in that case the details are typed on individual sheets after they have been 'run off'. When preparing the master (or draft) turn up nine single-line spaces after the date (leaving eight clear) before typing the salutation.
(b) Very often the name and address of addressee are not inserted and, if this is so, no space need be left when the master is prepared. Turn up three single-line spaces after date.

Salutation—

(a) Dear—the remainder of the salutation is typed in when the name and address are inserted.
(b) Dear Sir, Dear Madam, Dear Sir(s), Dear Sir/Madam.

Signature—the person writing the letter may or may not sign it. If the writer is signing, type the complimentary close, etc., in the usual way. If the writer is not signing, type Yours faithfully and company's name* in the usual position, turn up two single-line spaces and type the name of the person writing the letter, then turn up two single-line spaces and type the designation.

* If the company's name is not being inserted, turn up two single-line spaces after Yours faithfully and type the name of the writer, then turn up two single-line spaces and type the writer's designation.

Ribbon control lever

This is usually on the front of your machine, on the right-hand side, immediately above the keyboard. The lever may be set in three (more on certain models) positions:

(a) Black—to type on the top half of the ribbon.
(b) Red—to type on the bottom half of the ribbon.
(c) White or stencil—disconnects the ribbon.

If a technique is faulty, check with the following list and carry out the remedial drill.

Faulty technique		*Remedy*
'Raised Capitals', caused by releasing shift key too soon.	^I may go.	Drills 4–12 page 15; drill 4–12 page 16.
Uneven left margin, caused by faulty carriage return.	I may go. I may go.	Return carriage sharply without looking up. Any 'Apply the keys you know' drill.
Heavy strokes, caused by not releasing keys quickly.	I may go. may	Bounce fingers off keys. Practise finger movement drills.
Omitting or inserting words (looked up from the copy).	I ∧ go	Eyes on copy always. Drills 1, 2, and 3, page 24 backwards.
Extra spaces, caused by your leaning on the space bar.	I may go.	Right thumb slightly above space bar. Drills 5–7 page 13.
Omitting spaces, caused by poor wrist position.	I maygo.	Say 'space' to yourself each time you tap space bar. Drills 5, 6, 7 page 13. Drills 26, 27, 28 page 19.
Hands out of position. Return fingers to home keys.	I ,au go.	Return fingers to home keys. Any 'Apply the keys you know' drill.
Turning letters around—eyes get ahead of fingers.	I may og.	Eyes on copy always. Say each letter aloud as you type. Any preceding drills.
Letters and spaces overlap from typing jerkily.	I may go	Remember the 'tick-tock' rhythm—see page 20. Say each letter softly to yourself. Any drills.

Accuracy/speed practice

Practice routine

1. Type a copy of the exercise.

2. Check and draw a loop around all errors.

3. Compare your errors with those shown above.

4. Practise the remedial drills.

5. Type as much of the exercise as you can in the time suggested.

6. If you made more than the stipulated number of errors, continue with the timed practice and aim for accuracy.

7. If your errors were below the tolerance given, type the exercise again (timed) and endeavour to type a little faster.

Accuracy/speed practice

Set margins at 25 Elite, 18 Pica

19 w.p.m.	One minute	Not more than one error

A/S.1 As those shoes are too small, you should take them   10

back and have them changed for the right size.   19

(S.I. 1.00)

1 | 2 | 3 | 4 | 5 | 6 | 7 | 8 | 9 | 10 |

Skill building

In exercises A and B, type each line or sentence three times. If time permits, complete your practice by typing each group of lines as it appears. Keep your eyes on the copy and return the carriage sharply.

Margins:
Elite 22—82
Pica 12—72

A.   Review alphabet keys

1.   Marjorie had just come back from Africa and had altered considerably, being now quite unrecognisable, except for her voice.

B.   Build speed on alternate-hand words

2. island visit girls lamb worn paid she hay men for but the me

3. formal usual their lend lame work may pen dog got did and us

4. The girls and the men got paid for their work on the island.

5. The lamb and the lame dog lay by the pen.   She may visit me.

Accuracy practice   30 w.p.m.   Six minutes   Not more than four errors

For this exercise change margins to Elite 18—90, Pica 10—75

A.56 Perhaps the most lovable and desirable quality which a	11
person can have is that of tolerance. It need not be inborn	23
but it can be acquired and developed. It can be described	35
as the quality which makes us able to see the point of view	47
of the other fellow, and which makes us always keep in mind	59
the fact that, however correct we may think our own opinion	71
of a thing to be, we still may be wrong. It is the decency	83
in us that concedes to others the right to have their own	94
views. It prevents us from meddling with what is no con-	105
cern of ours, and enables us to let others seek their own	116
happiness and salvation in their own way. It is a good	127
thing if we have tolerance, but if we feel we have not, we	138
should make an effort to acquire and cultivate it. As a	149
matter of fact, in our present age, it is a rare quality,	160
but if we strive to recognise its existence, we shall have	172
gone a long way towards acquiring it. (S.I. 1.33)	180

Speed building   45 w.p.m.   1½ minutes   Not more than three errors

S.15 I suggest that you should be left free to choose those	11
whom you would like to have to work with you on this job, as	23
I feel sure that in this way there would be no cause for	34
friction. Please think this over, and if you feel that it	46
would be of great help to you, I am quite ready to have a talk	57
with you with a view to finding the best way to proceed.	68

(S.I. 1.08)

1 | 2 | 3 | 4 | 5 | 6 | 7 | 8 | 9 | 10 | 11 | 12 |

In exercises A and B, type each line or sentence three times, saying the letters to yourself. If time permits, complete your practice by typing each group of lines as it appears. Keep your eyes on the copy and return the carriage sharply. Set left margin stop at 25 Elite, 18 Pica.

A. Review alphabet keys

1. It was emphasized that the very young juniors need extra food which cannot be quickly obtained.

Position of hyphen varies on different machines. Find it on your machine and practise drills

B. Practise ■ (hyphen) key—; finger

2. ;-; ;-; p-; p-;-; blue-grey, one-fifth, part-time,
3. Over one-third are part-time day-release students.
4. Her father-in-law asked for all-wool yellow socks.

No space before or after hyphen

Accuracy/speed practice   20 w.p.m.   One minute   Not more than one error

A/S.2 If you are good at figures, and are keen to have a   10
       job in our firm, we should like you to call on us.   20
                                         (S.I. 1.05)

A/S.3 I wish that you could have been with us on Tuesday   10
       to see the new office machines which were on view.   20
                                         (S.I. 1.15)

       1 | 2 | 3 | 4 | 5 | 6 | 7 | 8 | 9 | 10 |

Record your progress

Instructions for all RECORD YOUR PROGRESS exercises:

(a) Type ONCE as practice.
(b) Check for errors.
(c) With the assistance of your teacher, analyse your errors and carry out remedial work where necessary.
(d) Type as much of the passage as you can in the time allotted.
(e) Check and circle any errors.
(f) Record the number of words typed and the number of errors in the second typing.

Record your progress   One minute

R.1 I know you will be pleased to hear that Mr. Thomas   10
     joined the firm on a part-time basis. He was told   20
     they would like to give him a short trial. (S.I. 1.11)   28

       1 | 2 | 3 | 4 | 5 | 6 | 7 | 8 | 9 | 10 |

Subdivided column headings with block-style tabulation

If you use block-style tabulation, then it is not necessary to centre subdivided headings vertically or horizontally. Starting points for headings will be the left margin and the tab stops set for each column. All headings will start on the same horizontal line which will be the starting point for the deepest heading. Exercise 4 below is an example of block-style with subdivided headings blocked—compare the layout with that in exercise 3 on page 140.

4. Type the following table on A4 paper in double-line spacing. Centre the whole table vertically and horizontally on the paper. Use block style. Leave three spaces between columns.

WEEKLY METAL PRICE CHANGES

Metal	Latest price per ton	Change on week	Year ago	1960-1967	
				High	Low
	£	£	£	£	£
Aluminium ..	378.60	---	272.50	378.60	272.50
Antimony ..	1660.00	---	1035.00	1660.00	865.00
Copper ..	527.65	22.25*	950.00	1380.00	498.75
Nickel ..	1950.00	---	1596.00	1797.00	1414.00
Wolfram ..	42.00	---	21.75	48.00	21.00
Zinc	330.50	6.00*	655.00	910.00	302.60

* In both cases this was an increase in the price.

Footnotes

In the table above you will notice an asterisk after the figures 22.25 and 6.00. This refers to the footnote after the last horizontal line. The footnote reference in the body is always a superior character (see page 132) and may be a figure or sign (asterisk, etc.).

In the body of a document there is *no* space before the figure or sign. At the bottom there is one space *after* the figure or sign. If there is no asterisk on your typewriter, make one with x and hyphen (combination characters—see page 129).

Record your progress

5½ minutes

R.29　　There are few jobs around the home these days which are too　　12
heavy for a woman to tackle—provided that she has the right　　24
kind of tools. With the ever-increasing interest in do-it-　　36
yourself work, husbands and wives are tackling many jobs as a　　48
team, so tools have been specially developed to enable wives to　　60
take their share.　　63
It may still seem a little strange to some onlookers to see　　75
women cutting hedges, trimming lawns, building shelves, or drill-　　88
ing walls. In fact, these jobs now need to be no more arduous than　　101
cleaning floors or washing clothes—and for the same reason.　　113
It is the introduction and development of the electric motor　　125
which has made light work of all these tasks. More and more women　　138
are finding out that they can carry out their own home maintenance　　151
with power tools. The electric drill, with its range of attach-　　163
ments, is finding a place beside the vacuum-cleaner and the food-　　176
mixer instead of being relegated to the work-bench in the garage.　　189

(S.I. 1.34)

In exercises A, B, and C, type each line or sentence three times, saying the letters to yourself. If time permits, complete your practice by typing each group of lines as it appears. Keep your eyes on the copy and return the carriage sharply. Set left margin stop at 25 Elite, 18 Pica.

A. Review alphabet keys

1. A small quiet boy who lives next door to Jack came out of the gate and went down the zigzag path.

Position of ? varies on different machines. Find it on your machine and practise drills

B. Practise **?** key—; finger

Two spaces after ? at end of a sentence

2. Now? When? Where? May she? Must we? Will you?
3. Who said so? What is the time? Is it late? Why?

Depress left shift key

C. Practise **:** (colon) key—; finger

4. ;;; ::: ;;; a:; l:; s:; k:; d:; j:; f:; hj:; gf:;a
5. Delivery Period: One month. Price: Nett ex Works.

One space after colon

Accuracy/speed practice   21 w.p.m.   One minute   Not more than one error

A/S.4 We trust that the hints we gave for the removal of   10

stains will be found to be of great help to all of   20

you. (S.I. 1.09)   21

A/S.5 When are you coming to see us? We look forward to   10

hearing an up-to-date account about your trips out   20

East. (S.I. 1.24)   21

1 | 2 | 3 | 4 | 5 | 6 | 7 | 8 | 9 | 10 |

Record your progress   One minute

R.2 What time does your train get in? You should take   10

the following with you: tennis racket, golf clubs,   20

golf balls, strong shoes, rain-coat, and rucksack.   30

(S.I. 1.17)

1 | 2 | 3 | 4 | 5 | 6 | 7 | 8 | 9 | 10 |

Practise centring subdivided column headings

3. Study the following table and the notes given below. Then display the table on A4 paper in double-line spacing. Centre vertically and horizontally and insert leader dots.

PLANNED TRAFFIC - 1977

Commodity	Canal Traffic '000 tons		
	Atlantic to Pacific	Pacific to Atlantic	Total
Wheat	2,901	100	3,001
Coarse Grain	13,000	353	13,353
Sugar	1,934	3,536	5,470
Soya Beans	5,237	---	5,237
Pulp and Paper	815	2,475	3,290
Iron and Steel Manufacturing	1,650	7,248	8,898
Miscellaneous Ores	710	3,050	3,760
Coal	14,500	200	14,700
Chemicals	2,700	655	3,355

Centring of headings horizontally and vertically

In the above table, the heading 'Canal Traffic '000 tons' must be centred over the second, third and fourth columns. To do this, first find the centre point to these three columns as explained on page 97 (Centring of Headings over Columns) and then proceed as follows:

(a) Along the first horizontal line, mark only the scale points for the vertical lines which extend to the top horizontal line.
(b) Centre and type the heading 'Canal Traffic '000 tons'.
(c) Type the horizontal line underneath this heading, and along this line mark the scale-points for the vertical lines for each of the three columns beneath.
(d) Type the headings for these three columns.
(e) Centre the heading for the first column vertically on the heading already typed. Do this by counting the number of lines and spaces in the heading typed—in this case five—and from this number take the number of lines to be typed, e.g., first heading 1 line from 5 lines = 4. Divide by 2 = 2. With the alignment scale on 'Canal Traffic '000 tons' turn up 2 spaces and type the heading 'Commodity'.
(f) Type the horizontal line below the deepest headings.
(g) The items in the first column (usually descriptive) all start at the same scale-point.
(h) In the figure columns, the longest figure is centred and other figures typed so that units are under units, tens under tens, etc.

Note: When ruling vertical lines for the subdivided columns, only extend these as far as the mark you have made on the second horizontal line as shown above. Always type the deepest heading first.

In exercises A and B, type each line or sentence three times, saying the letters to yourself. If time permits, complete your practice by typing each group of lines as it appears. Keep your eyes on the copy and return the carriage sharply. Set left margin stop at 25 Elite, 18 Pica.

A. Review alphabet keys

1. In spite of the likely hazard, a decision was made
   to grant their request and give him the extra job.

Shift-lock key

When you need to type several capital letters one after the other, the shift lock must be used. When this is depressed, you will be able to type capitals without using the shift key.

The following steps should be practised:
(a) Depress shift lock, using 'A' finger of left hand.
(b) Type capital letters.
(c) Depress left-hand shift key to release shift lock.

B. Practise shift-lock key

2. BEFORE lunch please ring me in LUDLOW next MONDAY.

3. MEETINGS held in LONDON, LIVERPOOL and MANCHESTER.

4. Both LAURA and KATHLEEN were present at the party.

Accuracy/speed practice	22 w.p.m.	One minute	Not more than one error

A/S.6 We fear that we shall be away for some months, but   10
       we shall keep in touch with you and will write you   20
       very soon. (S.I. 1.09)   22

A/S.7 We want a first-class employee: one who has a good   10
       knowledge of accounts. She must be able to manage   20
       a section. (S.I. 1.32)   22

1 | 2 | 3 | 4 | 5 | 6 | 7 | 8 | 9 | 10 |

Record your progress
One minute

R.3 No extra charge will be made to them for a copy of   10
       the DAILY GAZETTE; but their accounts must be paid   20
       at the end of each month. Will this suit them? I   30
       would like a reply today. (S.I. 1.20)   35

1 | 2 | 3 | 4 | 5 | 6 | 7 | 8 | 9 | 10 |

Leader dots

Leader dots (full stops) are used to guide the eye along lines of figures from one column to another. There are four methods of grouping which can be used, viz.
(a) One dot three spaces . . . .
(b) Two dots three spaces .. .. ..
(c) Three dots two spaces ... ...
(d) Continuous dots ....

The best grouping is the second, i.e., two dots and three spaces.
i Type leader dots lightly and evenly.
ii If any item in the column takes more than one line, the leader dots should be typed only on the last line of the item.

iii Care must be taken to see that the groups of dots come underneath one another in all lines. To ensure this, you should adopt the following procedure:
Bring carriage to the first tab stop.
Back-space for every space between first and second columns plus two extra spaces. Set a tab stop.
Back-space five from the tab stop just set and set another tab stop.
Continue in this way until you have approximately reached the last word of the shortest line in particulars column.
Bring carriage back to margin and type first line, using tab bar to insert leader dots if and where required.

Note: There must always be at least one space between the last word and the first group of dots or the last dot and the vertical line, i.e., leader dots must never be typed right up to the preceding or following word or line, and no word or letter must be allowed to extend beyond the last leader dot on the line, although leader dots may extend beyond the last word.

Practise typing tables with leader dots

1. Type the following table on A5 landscape paper (210 × 148 mm) and in double-line spacing, leaving three spaces between the columns. Centre vertically and horizontally. Use block or centred style with closed sides. Insert leader dots.

FINANCIAL SUMMARY IN £ STERLING

	1975	1974
Group Sales	48 168 000	42 506 400
Profit before Tax	5 229 400	3 685 100
Profit after Tax to Ordinary Shareholders	1 947 300	1 203 400
Profit retained in the business	497 300	380 000
Exports and Overseas Business	8 221 945	6 926 300

2. Type the following table on A5 portrait paper in double-line spacing. Centre horizontally and vertically. Use block or centred style. Insert leader dots.

COMPARISON OF SALES FIGURES IN £000

Details	1977	1976
Home sales	10,560	11,480
Exports	15,490	14,220
Subsidiaries	1,500	1,965
Tool sales	27,550	27,665
Trading Profit ..	2,072	3,414
Investment income	240	220
Bank interest ...	1,565	1,240

In exercises A and B, type each line or sentence three times, saying the letters to yourself. If time permits, complete your practice by typing each group of lines as it appears. Keep your eyes on the copy and return the carriage sharply. Set left margin stop at 25 Elite, 18 Pica.

A. Review alphabet keys

1. The boy did just give a quick answer but could not find words to explain the amazing story.

B. Practise ▇ (dash key) —; finger

— key
Practise ; to —
back to ;. Keep
first finger over
home key

2. ; - ; ; - ; Call today - no tomorrow - before tea. ONE space *before* and *after* dash

3. The book - it was his first - was a great success.

4. It is their choice - we are sure it will be yours.

Upper and lower case characters

Characters requiring use of shift key are called UPPER CASE characters.
Characters not requiring use of shift key are called LOWER CASE characters.

Accuracy/speed practice   23 w.p.m.   One minute   Not more than one error

A/S.8 If you feel some day that you would like a trip in   10
the country, perhaps you could drive out to a farm   20
to pick fruit. (S.I. 1.09)   23

A/S.9 Do you wish to take a holiday? Now is the time to   10
take one of our out-of-season vacations. Send for   20
our brochure. (S.I. 1.26)   23

    1 | 2 | 3 | 4 | 5 | 6 | 7 | 8 | 9 | 10 |

Record your progress   One minute

R.4 The goods which Mrs. Law saw last June are not now   10
in stock, and we shall not be able to replace them   20
for some weeks - perhaps a month - when we hope to   30
receive a further supply. (S.I. 1.17)   35

    1 | 2 | 3 | 4 | 5 | 6 | 7 | 8 | 9 | 10 |

Skill building

Type exercises A and B three times. Keep your eyes on the copy and return the carriage sharply.

Margins:
Elite 22—82
Pica 12—72

A. Review alphabet keys

1.   The jubilant Works Manager had no qualms about the boys going on the excursion in spite of the very freezing remarks made by the directors.

B. Improve control of vowel keys

2. superintendent approximately hesitated replied second before

3. unintelligible inconvenience evidently amounts colour differ

4. His remarks to the superintendent were unintelligible, and I hesitated for approximately a second before making my reply.

Accuracy Practice   30 w.p.m.   5½ minutes   Not more than five errors

Change margins to Elite 18—90, Pica 10—75

A.55   At the start of the year your Board was faced with a   **10**
strike of workers—trade union men who objected to the   **21**
employment by us of certain non-union men. We had to bow   **33**
to the wishes of the Union and accept the principle of the   **44**
'closed shop'. Later in the year we suffered from the   **55**
Government's policy and from the shortage of raw materials   **67**
caused by the dislocation of imports.   **75**

From the Balance Sheet you will see that our financial   **86**
position is sound. During the year we offered 50,000 unissued   **98**
£1 Ordinary Shares to the public; all were taken up, and this   **110**
provided us with capital that can now be used for the future   **122**
development of your Company. Bearing in mind all the problems   **135**
I feel sure you will be pleased with the recommendation of   **147**
your Board that a dividend of 12½ per cent be paid to holders   **159**
of the 150,000 Ordinary Shares.   **(S.I. 1.40)**   **165**

Speed building   45 w.p.m.   One minute   Not more than two errors

S.13   When you take your first job, make up your mind to save   **11**
a small sum, say 10 per cent, out of your salary each week.   **23**
In a few years you should have saved a large sum, and a time   **35**
may come when you will be glad you took my advice. **(S.I. 1.07)**   **45**

S.14   You must bear in mind that we all have to live and work   **11**
with other people and we should do our best not just for our   **23**
own good, but also for that of our neighbours. We should at   **35**
all times be ready to help those who are in need. **(S.I. 1.11)**   **45**

1 | 2 | 3 | 4 | 5 | 6 | 7 | 8 | 9 | 10 | 11 | 12 |

Tabulator key

Frequently, the first line of a paragraph starts five spaces to the right of the following lines. This is called 'indenting'. All machines have three tabulator controls which you should locate on your machine as their position varies on the different makes:

(a) A tab-set key to fix the tab stop
(b) A tab-clear key, to clear tab stops
(c) A tabulator bar, or key, to move the carriage to wherever a tab stop is set.

To indent a paragraph you must:
(a) Check that margins are set correctly.
(b) Clear all previous tab stops. On most machines this can be done by pressing the clear key while returning the carriage. On other machines there are special devices for this purpose.
(c) Return carriage. Indent five spaces and then firmly depress tab-set key.
(d) Test your setting by returning carriage and then depressing tabulator bar or key.

Practise paragraph indenting

Type the following paragraphs setting tab stop for indenting five spaces.

1.   We are sure you will already have noticed the effect of tax on a large number of the goods you see in shops, on some of which the tax has been reduced.

2.   We would like you to come and see the range of gifts on display at any one of our branches in the country, and shall be delighted to help you to select those that appeal to you.

Line-space regulator

In previous exercises you have been typing in 'single' spacing—the line-space regulator has been set on '1'. You can also type in double (one clear space between each line of typing) or treble spacing (two clear spaces between each line of typing).*

		Single spacing (type on every line)	Double spacing (type on every second line)	Treble spacing (type on every third line)
6 single-line spaces equal 25 mm (1 inch)	25 mm	I am going to the market today	I am (space) going (space) to (space)	I am (space) (space) going (space) (space)

* Most machines have half spacing, and the markings vary on different makes of machines, e.g., '2' may equal $1\frac{1}{2}$ or 2. *Check your machine.*

Practise line-spacing

Type the following paragraph first in single-line spacing and then in double-line spacing. Set tab stop for indenting five spaces.

3.   The line-space regulator - a lever at the left-hand end of the carriage - controls the distance between the lines of typing. It can be set for single, double or treble spacing.

Note use of the hyphen and dash

Checking appointments

Many secretaries are responsible for keeping and checking their employer's appointment diary. When appointments are entered, in addition to the date, time, and name of caller, it is helpful to have, if possible, some information as to the nature of the appointment. At the beginning of each day's work, the secretary should check with her boss his appointments for that day. She should ask if any special documents or other items will be required for each appointment. She will then get all the materials together, neatly and properly arranged in separate folders. It is a good plan to include a sheet or sheets of lined paper with the date and name of caller typed at the top. This will be most useful for the boss for making notes. The competent secretary is always anticipating her employer's needs.

Review Quiz No. 6

1. An invoice is a document sent from the . . . to the . . .

2. A trader registered for VAT must issue a . . . invoice.

3. To reimburse a customer for goods returned a . . . . . . is usually issued.

4. A statement of account is a . . . of a month's transactions.

5. The marginal correction sign to denote capital letters is . . . and to denote small letters . . .

6. To type a brace use . . . . . .

7. Square brackets are formed by using the . . . and . . .

8. For an asterisk, if this is not provided on a machine, use small . . . and . . .

9. For the Roman numeral ONE always use . . . . . ., never . . . . . .

10. Inferior characters are typed . . . the writing line.

11. Superior characters are typed . . . the writing line.

12. Leave . . . spaces after a full stop at the end of a sentence.

13. . . . space is left before but . . . space after a comma, semicolon or colon.

14. . . . space is left before or after a hyphen.

15. . . . space is left . . . and . . . space after a dash.

16. Spacing after punctuation must always be . . .

17. . . . salutation is used in memoranda.

Turn to page 151 and check your answers. Score one point for each correct entry.
Total score: 29

Skill building

For all Skill Building exercises use A4 paper (210 × 297 mm)

In exercises A, B and C, type each line or sentence three times. If time permits, complete your practice by typing each group of lines as it appears. Keep your eyes on the copy and return the carriage sharply.

A.   Review alphabet keys

Left margin: Elite 25
Pica 18

1.   Agatha wears the most beautiful and exquisite
necklace of topaz and jade that Kay has ever seen.

B.   Practise figure 1 —L finger *

* If use of figure 1 is preferred, use A finger

Use small 'L' for figure 1

2. We require 11 pairs size 11, also 11 pairs size 1.

3. Add up 1 plus 11 plus 11 plus 11 plus 11 plus 111.

4. They have 111 pairs of size 11 socks for 111 boys.

C.   Practise figure 2 and " key—S finger

Practise S to W to 2 back to S

5. sw2s sw2s s2ws s2ws 2 seas 2 sons 2 sets 22 ships.

6. Send 2 grey, 2 red, 2 gold, 2 white, also 2 green.

7. sw"s sw"s w"ws w"ws "2" "22" "12" "21" "The Times"

Depress right shift key for "

NO space after initial " and NO space before closing "

8. "Go for 12 days."   "Come at 12 noon."   "Call now."

Accuracy/speed practice   24 w.p.m.   One minute   Not more than one error

A/S.10   When you leave the office at night you should   9
make sure that your machine is covered up and that   19
your desk is quite clear. **(S.I. 1.12)**   24

A/S.11   Your account for June should now be paid, and   9
I must ask you to let me have a cheque for the sum   19
due as soon as possible. **(S.I. 1.12)**   24

        1 | 2 | 3 | 4 | 5 | 6 | 7 | 8 | 9 | 10 |

Record your progress   One minute

R.5   Our parents are fond of telling us that, when   9
they were young, they had to work much harder than   19
we do now - but we shall, no doubt, tell our chil-   29
dren the same thing some day. **(S.I. 1.11)**   35

        1 | 2 | 3 | 4 | 5 | 6 | 7 | 8 | 9 | 10 |

UNIT 25   33

Type the following invoice on a suitable form.

FROM: The Universal Supply Co. Ltd., 84–114 High Street, Aberdeen. AB2
3HE Invoice No. 3843 dated 17th May 1977 VAT Ref. No. 992 3872 78

TO: H. Williamson & Co. 25 North Street Montrose Angus DD10 8AA
Terms: Nett 30 days
Tax Point: 17.5.77 Type of supply: Sale VAT 25%
Goods supplied: 5 Lightweight Steam Irons @ £11.20 ea. £56.00 (VAT £14.00)
             4 Electric Coffee Grinders @ £5.69 ea. £22.76 (VAT £5.69)
             6 Electric Carpet Sweepers @ £80 ea. £480.00 (VAT £120.00)
Total goods £558.76 Total VAT £139.69 Total amount due £698.45

Job 36   Production Target—eleven minutes

Type the following exercise on A4 paper making the corrections where indicated. Use double-line spacing, suitable margins, and indented paragraphs.
Insert heading COUNTY BOUNDARY CHANGES — *Local Government Act*

The Local Govt Act of 1972 changed the names & boundaries
of a number of counties in Scotland, England & Wales, &, as
county names normally form part of the postal address, the Post
Office hv asked customers to use the new counties. To avoid
confusion, the PO hv said th the counties of Greater Manchester
and Hereford & Worcester shd not be used. Towns in these new
counties shd be addressed in the same way as previously. [It shd
be noted th only the county names hv changed, & th the Post
Towns (i.e., towns to which mail is routed for delivery) &
Postcodes hv not changed, *or altered*.

Post Towns are an important part of the postal system & on
envelopes (or on the letter if a window envelope is being
used) shd always be typed in caps. If you do not know the
correct Post Town for a particular address, check in the
Post Office Guide or w yr local PO. *on a fresh line and* *The county, however, must be in lower case w. initial capital.*

Record your progress   5 minutes

For this exercise change margins to Elite 18–90, Pica 10–75

R.28		
A good dictionary is the most useful reference book you	11
can have. It is a tool to help you to do your work well and	23
easily, but, like all tools, it must be handled correctly if	35
the best use is to be made of it. All words are arranged in	47
alphabetical order of the first letter of the word, and then	59
according to the second, third, and remaining letters. Thus	71
'band' will come before 'bay'. A short word always appears	83
before a longer word; thus 'bind' will come before 'binder'	94
and 'found' before 'founder'. You must be sure you know how	106
your dictionary shows and uses hyphens; take care not to mix	118
up the use of the hyphen to join compound words, and its use	130
for dividing words or syllables. Remember to keep your dic-	142
tionary always at hand, ready for use, and, when you are	153
doubtful about the spelling or meaning of a word, look it up.	165

(S.I. 1.33)

Technique development

Sizes of type faces

The two most usual type faces are: ELITE   PICA

. . . .

Standard sizes of paper

In the office you will have to use different sizes of paper. The standard sizes are known as the 'A' series and are shown below. The most common of these sizes are: A4, A5, and A6.

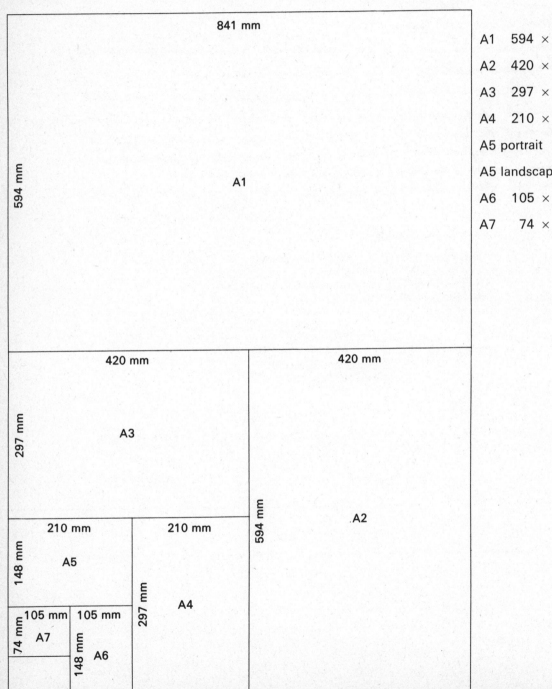

Sizes

A1 594 × 841 mm

A2 420 × 594 mm

A3 297 × 420 mm

A4 210 × 297 mm

A5 portrait 148 × 210 mm

A5 landscape 210 × 148 mm

A6 105 × 148 mm

A7   74 × 105 mm

Type the following letter on A4 paper and take one carbon copy. Address an envelope of suitable size. Insert today's date.

Our Ref HMS/TUR

Miss D. F Hughes Bakewell Rd Matlock Derbyshire DE4 3AP

Dear Madam Sailings to Australia

NP Thank you f yr ltr dated (insert suitable date). [The following passenger liners wl leave from Southampton on the dates given below:

set LINERS

Glen More   23rd April

Glen Nevis   16th May

Glen Isla   20th July

May we point out th return tickets (wh are cheaper than the single fares) are valid for 18 mths fr the date of departure to the date of embarkation on the final stage of the return journey. The full fare for both outward and return journeys must be pd before the start of the initial journey. [We enclose a booklet giving booking information. Please do not hesitate to contact us if there are any points on wh you are not clear.

Yrs ffy GLEN SHIPPING CO LTD   HM SYLVESTER Manager

Display the following on A5 paper.

Double Discount Week (closed caps and underscore)
Prices are rising—save £££'s (underscore)
                    BUY NOW (spaced caps and underscore)
Television Sets—Black and White   £45—£100
                    Colour   £150—£250
Carpet Sweepers   £40—£60
Dish Washers   £90—£300
Sewing Machines   £50—£260
                    Discount normally 5%
                    THIS WEEK 10%

Type the following table on A5 landscape paper and rule. Use double spacing for the body. Type in block or centred style.

C A R P E T   S A L E

Size		Content	Price/Medium Domestic
			£
9' × 12'	2.74 m × 3.66 m	Wool	140.99
12' × 12'	3.66 m × 3.66 m	Wool/Nylon	120.95
12' × 15'	3.66 m × 4.57 m	Viscose/Nylon	110.75
12' × 21'	3.66 m × 6.40 m	Wool	160.99
15' × 21'	4.57 m × 6.40 m	Acrylic	190.10

Horizontal display

For centring a line in the full width of the paper, take the following steps:

(a) See that the left edge of paper is at 0 on the carriage-position scale.
(b) Move margin stops to extreme left and right.
(c) Divide by 2 the total number of spaces between 0 and the scale-point reached by the right-hand edge of paper; this gives the centre point of paper.
(d) Bring carriage to centre point of paper.
(e) Locate the back-space key (top left or top right of keyboard) and from the point reached in (d) back-space once for every two letters and spaces in the heading. Ignore any odd letter left over.
(f) Start to type the heading at the point reached.

Number of spaces to 25 mm (1")

Elite—12   Pica—10

Number of horizontal spaces in full width of the paper sizes A4 and A5

	Elite	Pica	Centre Point:	Elite	Pica
A4 paper (210 × 297 mm)	100	82		50	41
A5 landscape paper (210 × 148 mm)	100	82		50	41
A5 portrait paper (148 × 210 mm)	70	59		35	29

Practise horizontal centring

1. Centre the following headings on a sheet of A5 landscape paper in double spacing. Remember to see that the left edge of paper is at 0 on carriage-position scale. NO punctuation should be typed after a heading unless the last word is abbreviated, when a full stop is used.

Winter Holidays

Spring Sale

Win a Television Recorder

Major Oil Find

Financial Planning

Market Research Co.

Check, by measuring, that you have the same space on the left as on the right of the headings.

2. Type the following on A5 landscape paper (210 × 148 mm) in double-line spacing, centring each line horizontally. No punctuation should be typed at the end of a line unless the last word is abbreviated. Turn down 12 single-line spaces from the top edge of paper.

Shorthand-Typist

required for

Sales Manager

Apply by letter to

Personnel Officer

Midland Motors Ltd.

Worcester Street, Hereford

Type the following exercises in double-line spacing on a sheet of A4 paper. Use suitable margins. In the body, the words underlined should be typed as shoulder headings.

POSTFAX

A Post Office Service

Postfax is a service that enables y to send an exact copy of a doc. fr one Post Office to another. At present the service is available at Post Offices in the major business centres throughout the U.K. in full please.

Transmission

Hand in the doc at a P.O. It will be fed into a machine which transmits the image via the telephone system to a machine at a P.O. in the city of destination. The receiving P.O. wl deliver then the copy to a given address or it may be collected.

Sizes of Documents

You can send any doc. up to a max. size of 14" (355.6 mm) × 8½" (215.9 mm).

(a) Type the following form letter on A5 paper. Take one carbon copy.

```
                   A D PERRY LTD
                   37 East Cliff
             PRESTON, Lancs      PR1 3JN


Our Ref
(Turn up 12 single-line spaces)



Dear

Please send us your prices and terms for the following:
(Turn up 12 single-line spaces)



Yours faithfully
A D PERRY LTD
```

(b) On the carbon copy insert:
Our Ref *Pur/JH* To: *G F Jukes Ltd 19 Wellington Rd*
Stockport Cheshire SK1 3UQ
Dear *Sirs* Prices and terms required for:
5 Clerical Teak Desks 150 mm × 635 mm × 762 mm
2 Secretarial Teak Desks 125 mm × 762 mm × 762 mm
2 Secretarial Posture Chairs (Adjustable) 431 mm × 533 mm × 700 mm

In exercises A, B and C, type each line or sentence three times. If time permits, complete your practice by typing each group of lines as it appears. Keep your eyes on the copy and return the carriage sharply.

A.   Review alphabet keys

Left margin: Elite 25
Pica 18

1.   The junior office clerks were quite amazed at the extra reward given by their generous employer.

Practise D to
E to 3 back to D

B.   Practise 3 and / (solidus) key—D finger

2. de3d de3d d3ed d3ed 3 days 3 dogs 3 desks 33 dolls

3. Order 3 sets of 3 for 33 High Street, not 33 sets.

NO space before or after /

Depress right
shift key for /

4. de/d de/d d/ed d/ed 1/32 his/hers is/as not yes/no

5. "Call at 13/23 West Street."   "Ask him/her to go."

Practise F to R to
4 back to F

C.   Practise 4 and @ key—F finger

6. fr4f fr4f f4rf f4rf 4 fees 4 fans 44 figs 44 files

7. There will be 4 men, 4 women, 4 girls and 44 boys.

8. fr@f fr@f f@rf f@rf 4 @ 44 and 44 @ 4 also 44 @ 44

Depress right
shift key for @

Leave ONE space before and after @

9. "Buy 4 @ 34/44."   "Send 2 @ 14/24 to 4 East Road."

Accuracy/speed practice   25 w.p.m.   One minute   Not more than one error

A/S.12   We have just moved to our new house, and when   9
we have put it straight we shall be pleased if you   19
will spend a few days with us. (S.I. 1.00)   25

A/S.13   I am delighted to tell you that I have joined   9
the team now.   I had hoped to do so last year, but   19
they considered I was too young. (S.I. 1.16)   25

1 | 2 | 3 | 4 | 5 | 6 | 7 | 8 | 9 | 10 |

Record your progress   One minute

R.6   I am sorry to hear that my cheque - sent last   9
month - has not yet been received; I think it must   19
have gone astray in the post. Shall I ask my bank   29
to stop payment? I can then forward another.   38
(S.I. 1.18)

1 | 2 | 3 | 4 | 5 | 6 | 7 | 8 | 9 | 10 |

UNIT 27   **36**

Production typing

Job 28   Production Target—ten minutes

Type the following exercise on A5 landscape paper. Use suitable margins and single-line spacing.

<u>MEASUREMENTS</u>

When using 'x' (always small 'x') for the multiply sign, leave <u>one</u> space either side of the 'x', e.g., 20 (space) ft (space) x (space) 10 (space) ft = 20 ft x 10 ft. The same spacing is necessary when using Metric Measurements, e.g., 1 m = 100 cm; 1 m = 1000 mm; 1 m x 1000 = 1 km.

You can also use the sign for feet and inches, e.g., 20 ft 10 in x 15 ft 9 in = 20' 10" x 15' 9". You will see that, when using the sign, there is no space between the figure and the sign, but there is one space after the sign.

Do not add 's' to the plural of ft, in, lb, m, kg, etc. In Imperial Measurements a full stop may be used after an abbreviation, but in Metric Measurements full stops are <u>never</u> used after the symbols except at the end of a sentence, e.g., 210 mm x 297 mm.

Job 29   Production Target—eight minutes

Type the following exercise on suitable memo paper. Type the word <u>CONFIDENTIAL</u> in top left-hand corner.

To: Miss P. Jackson (Personnel)   Date: 21st August, 1977

From: J. Hayward   Subject: Secretary to Managing Director

Further to my tel. conversation on Tuesday last, I confirm th. Mr. Howard-Smith's Sec. wl be leaving at the end of Sept. + th a replacement wl be required on 1st Oct.

The person appointed shd be over 25 years of age + shd hv the following min. qualifications:

LCC Private Secretary's Diploma

( ) 2 GCE 'A' Levels (Preferably English + German) suitable

H When y hv short listed 3 candidates, pse. let me know + I wl arrange for Mr. Howard-Smith to interview them.

Technique development

Vertical display

Notices, dance tickets, programmes, and similar display matter, should occupy a central position on the paper, both horizontally and vertically. You have already learned how to centre horizontally, now you will learn how to centre matter vertically. There are 6 single-line spaces to 1 inch (25 mm) so that the number of single-line spaces to a page is as follows: A4 (210 × 297 mm) = 70; A5 landscape (210 × 148 mm) = 35; A5 portrait (148 × 210 mm) = 50.

To centre matter vertically on a sheet of paper, take the following steps:

1. Find the number of single-line spaces on the paper.
2. Count the number of lines and blank spaces between the lines on the copy.
3. Deduct 2 from 1.
4. Divide answer in 3 by 2 to equalize top and bottom margins (ignore fractions).
5. Insert paper with left edge at 0 on paper scale. See that top edge of paper is level with alignment scale.
6. Turn up number of spaces arrived at in 4 plus 1 extra space.
7. Centre and type first line of display.

Practise horizontal and vertical display

Display the following notice on A5 landscape paper (210 × 148 mm), each line to be centred horizontally and the whole notice vertically. The vertical spacing at the side of the notice and the calculation below the notice are given as a guide.

Line 1	OUTSTANDING VALUE OFFERED IN
Space	
Space	
Line 2	Filing Folders
Space	
Line 3	Letter Racks
Space	
Line 4	Document Wallets
Space	
Line 5	Filing Cabinets
Space	
Line 6	Duplicating Paper

Vertical display

1. Number of lines on paper (210 × 148 mm) = 35
2. Number of lines and spaces in copy = 12
3. Deduct (2) from (1) 35–12 = 23
4. Divide answer in (3) by 2 for top and bottom margins (ignore fraction) 23 ÷ 2 = 11
5. Turn up 12 single-line spaces and type first line of notice

Horizontal display

Check that paper is at 0 on paper scale. Bring carriage to centre point of paper (50 Elite, 41 pica). Back-space once for every 2 letters and spaces in each line.

		Elite	Pica
Line 1 begins at		36	27
2	„ „	43	34
3	„ „	44	35
4	„ „	42	33
5	„ „	43	34
6	„ „	42	33

Technique development

Typing 'off the line'

Superior (raised) characters
Turn the paper *down* half a single-line space and type the character to be raised. If your machine does not have half-spacing, use the interliner.

$$10° C \qquad a^2 - b^2$$

Superior characters are used for typing degrees and mathematical formulae.

Inferior (lowered) characters
Turn the paper *up* half a single-line space and type the character to be lowered. If your machine does not have half-spacing, use the interliner.

$$H_2O \qquad C_{12}H_{22}O_{11}$$

Inferior characters are used for typing chemical formulae.

Practise typing superior and inferior characters

1. Type each of the following lines three times in double spacing on A5 landscape paper.

Inferior characters are used in H_2SO_4, $CaCO_3$, H_2O and CO_2.

Superior characters are used for typing degrees, i.e., 29°.

A right angle equals 90°; 1° equals 60', and 1' equals 60".

At 1400 hours their position was 52° 30' N. and 15° 30' W.

Roman numerals

Practise typing Roman numerals

2. Study the following table; then type it on memo. paper, centring the numbers under the headings.

Arabic	Capital Roman	Small Roman	Arabic	Capital Roman	Small Roman
1	I	i	20	XX	xx
2	II	ii	30	XXX	xxx
3	III	iii	40	XL	xl
4	IV	iv	50	L	l
5	V	v	60	LX	lx
6	VI	vi	70	LXX	lxx
7	VII	vii	80	LXXX	lxxx
8	VIII	viii	90	XC	xc
9	IX	ix	100	C	c
10	X	x	500	D	d
			1000	M	m

Use capital I for Roman numeral one

Note and practise the use of Roman numerals

3. Study the following. Then with suitable display, arrange it as a notice on A5 landscape paper.

Use of roman numerals
(a) For designation of Monarchs, Form and Class Numbers.
  Examples: George VI   Form V   Class IX
(b) For numbering of Tables or Paragraphs instead of using ordinary (Arabic) figures.
  Examples: Chapter IX   Table XII
(c) Sometimes to express the year.
  Example: 1962   MCMLXII
(d) Small Roman numerals are used for numbering prefaces of books or sub-paragraphs or sub-sections.

Practise typing Roman numerals

4. Type the following exercise on A5 landscape paper in double-line spacing, once for practice, once for speed, and finally once for accuracy.

The boys in Forms VI and IX will take Stages I, II, and III.
Charles II, Henry VIII, George IV, James VI, and Edward III.
Refer to Section IX, Chapter II, Page 340, Paragraph 1(iii).
Read parts XVI, XVII, and XVIII, sub-sections ii, vi, and x.

UNIT 87

In exercises A, B and C, type each line or sentence three times. If time permits, complete your practice by typing each group of lines as it appears. Keep your eyes on the copy and return the carriage sharply.

A. Review alphabet keys

Left margin:
22 Elite
12 Pica

1.   The taxi driver whizzed along the busy road and a small girl jumped quickly back to safety.

B. Practise 7 and & (ampersand) key—J finger

Practise J to U to 7 back to J

2. ju7j ju7j j7uj j7uj 7 jars 7 jets 7 jigs 77 jacks 77 jellies

3. These 7 boys and 7 girls sent 7 plates and 7 dishes to them.

Depress left shift key for &

4. ju&j ju&j j&uj j&uj 1 & 2, 2 & 3, 3 & 4, 4 & 7, 7 & 17 & 27.

Leave ONE space before and after &

5. Let Jones & Co. at 7 & 77 High Street have 77 jars of honey.

C. Practise 8 and ' (apostrophe) key—K finger

Practise K to I to 8 back to K

6. ki8k ki8k k8ik k8ik 8 keys 8 kits 88 kids 88 kilts 88 kings;

7. About 8 men, 8 women, 8 girls and 8 boys went on the outing.

NO space before or after ' in middle of word

Depress left shift key for '

8. ki'k ki'k k'ik k'ik It's Joe's job. Dad's car. Mary's dog.

9. Bill's 8 vans are with John's 8 trucks at 87/88 King's Road.

Accuracy/speed practice	25 w.p.m. 1½ minutes	Not more than two errors

A/S.14   A year ago I said that you should be given a trial as a   **11**
clerk in sales and, as one of the staff will be leaving next   **23**
week, I would like you to take his place. Let me know if it   **35**
suits you. (S.I. 1.11)   **37**

A/S.15   Thank you for your note regarding the desks we ordered.   **11**
These are not required right away but if you can let us have   **23**
them by Tuesday of next week, we will send you our cheque by   **35**
return of post. (S.I. 1.18)   **38**

1 | 2 | 3 | 4 | 5 | 6 | 7 | 8 | 9 | 10 | 11 | 12 |

Record your progress   One minute

R.7   There must be little imps who sleep until one begins to   **11**
work and then they come to our office and start to worry and   **23**
try us. Some of you may find it hard sometimes to keep your   **35**
mind on the work you are doing, but you must learn to do so.   **47**
(S.I. 1.15)

1 | 2 | 3 | 4 | 5 | 6 | 7 | 8 | 9 | 10 | 11 | 12 |

Skill building

Type exercises A and B three times. Keep your eyes on the copy and return the carriage sharply.

A. Review alphabet keys

Margins: Elite 22—82
Pica 12—72

1. His extra blazer was made of the finely woven jet black cloth, and a quaint colourful badge adorned the pocket.

B. Improve control of figure keys

2. we 23 24 25 26 27 28 29 30 31 32 33 34 35 36 37 38 39 40 41.

3. Order Nos. 2981/76 & 2995/76 were sent on 31st August, 1976.

4. Cheque No. 021048 is for £536.97 and No. 021069 for £534.78.

Accuracy practice   30 w.p.m.   Five minutes   Not more than five errors

Note: From now on you must make your own line-end divisions when typing Accuracy Practice and Record your Progress exercises. For these exercises use margins of: Elite 18—90, Pica 10—75.

A.54 For some reason, I have been unable to obtain any satis-	11
faction from you in connection with the clock I left with you	23
3 months ago to be repaired. At that time, I pointed out to	35
you that the clock was not in first-class condition when I	47
bought it. Right from the beginning, it has always lost about	59
8 minutes every day.	63
From time to time I have telephoned your company about	74
the clock, and I usually spoke to Mr. G. Slown. A week ago	85
Mr. Slown telephoned me and promised to let me know this	97
week, without fail, what could be done to settle this matter.	109
I do not wish to make the same complaint over and over	121
again, but I cannot understand why a firm as large as yours	133
should neglect to make some adjustments when one of its clocks	145
had not been satisfactory. (S.I. 1.33)	150

Speed building   40 w.p.m.   Two minutes   Not more than four errors

S.11 We learn from your wife that you hope to build a new	10
house soon. Before the work starts, be sure you know what	22
kind of wood will be used. Last week we sent you one of our	34
books, and we would like you to read the section on wood.	45
We feel sure you will find the book a great help. Do not	56
forget to let your agent know that you must have the kind	68
of wood we suggest, and that you insist on the best quality.	80
(S.I. 1.10)	
S.12 It is sad to think that it is so easy to believe false	11
tales about others, or what is known as scandal. Perhaps	22
there are few people who ever tell the real truth about	33
others, and when we seek to test the truth of a tale we have	45
heard we sometimes find it is not quite true. This may not	57
be because those who tell the tale mean harm. All they want	69
is to make life less humdrum and add some colour to it.	80
(S.I. 1.17)	

1 | 2 | 3 | 4 | 5 | 6 | 7 | 8 | 9 | 10 | 11 | 12 |

Technique development

Layout of notice

Before starting to print a notice, printers prepare a plan or 'layout'—a sketch showing the manner in which the matter is to be arranged and the number of lines to be occupied. You should do the same when typing a notice. Prepare your plan on paper in pencil, and keep it in front of you when you type the notice.

Always prepare a plan for display work

1. Prepare a plan and type the following notice on A5 landscape paper (210 × 148 mm). Centre each line horizontally and the whole notice vertically. The calculations below the notice are given as a guide.

Line 1   Line 2
NORTH DEVON FARM/offers Holiday Accommodation/
Line 3
Delightful situation/
Line 4
Good food, service and friendly atmosphere/
Line 5   Line 6   Line 7
Ideal for children// Write for Brochure to/J. Holmes/
Line 8
Home Farm, Barnstaple, North Devon

/ = Turn up 2 spaces (leaving one blank line)
// = Turn up 3 spaces (leaving 2 blank lines)

Vertical display

(a) Number of lines on paper (210 × 148 mm) = 35
(b) Number of lines and spaces in copy = 16
(c) Deduct (b) from (a) 35 − 16 = 19
(d) Divide (c) by 2 for top and bottom margins (ignore fraction) 19 ÷ 2 = 9
(e) Turn up 10 single-line spaces and type first line of notice.

Horizontal display

Check that paper is at 0 on paper scale. Bring to centre point (50 Elite 41 Pica). Back-space once for every 2 letters and spaces in each line.

	Elite	Pica
Line 1 begins at	42	33
2 " "	36	27
3 " "	40	31
4 " "	29	20
5 " "	41	32
6 " "	40	31
7 " "	46	37
8 " "	33	24

2. Prepare a plan and type the following notice on A5 portrait paper (148 × 210 mm). Centre each line horizontally and the whole notice vertically. Divide lines where suitable.

ANNUAL GENERAL MEETING of the Social Club

will be held on Friday 14th July

at 12 noon in the Main Hall. All members

are requested to attend.

The brace is used by printers for joining up two or more lines. To represent the brace in typing, we use continuous brackets as shown in Exercise 3 below.

Practise typing brace

3. Type the following on A5 portrait paper, centring horizontally and vertically. Use double spacing except for bracketed items which should be in single spacing. Leave three spaces between columns.

<u>CLASS LIST</u>

	Position	Marks
H. Jones	1	78
A. Adkins	2	76
F. Foster	3)	74)
G. Green	3)	74)
H. Hopkins	5)	70)
L. Jones	5)	70)
L. Lawson	5)	70)

4. Type the following on A5 landscape paper in block style. Use line-spacing as shown. Margins: Elite 22–82, Pica 12–72. Leave five spaces between columns.

<u>SPACING BEFORE AND AFTER PUNCTUATION</u>

Full stop	Two spaces at end of sentence	Spacing after punctuation marks must be consistent
Comma) Semicolon) Colon)	No space before, one space after	
Dash	One space before and one space after	
Hyphen	No space before and no space after	
Exclamation sign) Question mark)	No space before, two spaces after at end of sentence	

Record your progress   4½ minutes

R.27   Before your employer leaves on a business trip, obtain   11
from him clear instructions as to the kind of letters to be   23
sent on to him. Open all such letters except those marked   35
'Private'. If you send on the letters themselves, take copies   47
as a safeguard against loss in the post. When posting, make   59
sure that the package or envelope is addressed to the place   71
reached by your employer by the time it gets there. Mark the   82
package clearly 'To await arrival'. State the address to   94
which the package should be returned if it is not claimed   105
within a certain time. You should also always keep a record   117
of all correspondence you send, with the date of posting   128
and the address to which it was sent. Some employers like   140
to have a daily summary of all important letters. (S.I. 1.33)   150

    1 | 2 | 3 | 4 | 5 | 6 | 7 | 8 | 9 | 10 | 11 | 12 |

Skill building

In exercises A, B and C, type each line or sentence three times. If time permits, complete your practice by typing each group of lines as it appears. Keep your eyes on the copy and return the carriage sharply.

A.   Revise alphabet keys

Left Margin: 22 Elite
12 Pica

1.   The pilot was unable to land the jet owing to extremely thick fog which quite covered the whole zone.

B.   Practise **9** and **(** (parenthesis or bracket) key—L finger

Practise L to 0 to 9 back to L

2. lo9l lo9l 19ol 19ol 9 laws 9 legs 99 lids 99 locks 99 lakes.

3. Send 9 cups and 9 saucers, 9 plates, 19 knives and 19 forks.

Leave ONE space before (but NO space after

Depress left shift key for (

4. lo(l lo(l l(ol l(ol (9 (8 (7 (4 (lad (log (logs (load (loads

C.   Practise **0** and **)** key—; finger

Practise ; to P to 0 back to ,

5. ;p0; ;p0; ;0p; ;0p; 1900; 1930; 1940; 1980; 1970; 1090; 100;

6. ;p); ;p); ;)p; ;)p; 20); 30); 40); 74); 800); 390); ;0); ;0;

Depress left shift key for)

Leave NO space before) but ONE space after

7. (a) 9 pots; (b) 2 pans; (c) 3 sets; (d) 7 cakes; (e) 10 dogs

Accuracy/speed practice   25 w.p.m.   Two minutes   Not more than two errors

A/S.16   We were all happy to hear that you are now back at work   11
and we hope that the long rest by the sea will have restored   23
you to good health. As soon as you can, please call and see   35
us. You will notice that we have moved to a new house quite   47
near to the park. (S.I. 1.06)   50

A/S.17   We have not yet been able to send the goods you ordered   11
last week as they are not stock lines, but we will do all we   23
can to let you have some of the goods, if not all, by Friday   35
of next week. We trust you will excuse this slight delay in   47
making despatch. (S.I. 1.14)   50

      1 | 2 | 3 | 4 | 5 | 6 | 7 | 8 | 9 | 10 | 11 | 12 |

Record your progress   Two minutes

R.8   Have you and your family ever thought of taking an out-   11
of-season holiday? A winter break - early in the new year -   23
may be just what you need. In our brochures you will find a   35
wide choice of places to which you can fly. Ask for details   47
from: Sun Tours Ltd., Great North Road, Edinburgh. Write to   59
us straight away. (S.I. 1.23)   62

      1 | 2 | 3 | 4 | 5 | 6 | 7 | 8 | 9 | 10 | 11 | 12 |

Combination characters

Some characters not provided on the typewriter can be typed by combining two characters, i.e., by typing one character, back-spacing and then typing the second character, or by typing one character and then the second immediately afterwards. In some cases the interliner must be used to allow the characters to be slightly raised or lowered.

Study carefully the following examples:

Exclamation sign	!	Apostrophe and full stop.
Division sign	÷	Colon and hyphen.
Dollar sign	$	Capital S and solidus.
Asterisk	*	Small x and hyphen. (On your machine you may have to raise the hyphen or lower it slightly by means of the interliner.)
Equation sign	=	Two hyphens, one typed slightly above the other by using the interliner.
Brace (commonly called brackets)	( ) ( )	Continuous brackets.
Square brackets	[ ]	Solidus and underscore.

On many machines the asterisk and equation sign are provided.

Practise typing combination characters

1. Type each of the following lines three times on A5 landscape paper (210 × 148 mm) in double-line spacing.

From afar there came to our ears the call "Cuckoo! Cuckoo!"

They had spent $300 on presents and came home with only $50.

The asterisk (*) is used for a reference mark in a footnote.

250 ÷ 5 + 50 ÷ 4 = 25; 25 × 5 - 15 ÷ 2 = 55; $125 ÷ 5 = $25.

To type a square bracket take the following steps:

Left bracket (a) Type solidus sign;
(b) Backspace once and type underscore;
(c) Turn platen back one full single-line space and type underscore;
(d) Turn platen up one single-line space, backspace once and continue with typing up to the right bracket.

Right bracket: (a) Type solidus sign;
(b) Backspace 2 and type underscore;
(c) Turn platen back one full single-line space and type underscore;
(d) Turn platen up one single-line space, tap space-bar once, and continue with typing.

Practise typing square brackets

2. Type the following line 3 times on A5 landscape paper in double-line spacing.

[756 ÷ 12 = 63] [12 × 5 = 60] [20 ÷ 2 = 10 + 15 - 25 + 10]

Technique development

Learn to respond to margin bell

Five to six spaces from the right margin a bell on your machine will ring to warn you that you are almost at the end of the writing line. When the bell rings, you must quickly decide whether you can finish the word on the line, or whether to hyphenate it and carry part of the word to the next line. The object of dividing a word at the end of a line is to avoid an uneven right margin.

If you must divide a word, then
(a) Divide according to syllables
    per-fect, under-stand
(b) Never carry two letters only to next line
    aid*ed*, ear*ly*
(c) Always type hyphen at end of line
    doubt-ing
(d) Never divide words pronounced as one syllable
    strength, passed

Practise line-end division of words

1. Type the following paragraphs once for practice and then once for accuracy. Use A5 landscape paper (210 × 148 mm) and double-line spacing. Set margins at Elite 22–82, Pica 12–72. Paragraph indentation 5.

We have an opening for a general works inspector, whose duties will consist chiefly of supervising, under the direction of the Clerk of Works, contractors experienced in highway and main drainage projects.

Applicants are expected to have dealt with engineering contracts for some years. Apart from the usual holiday pay, benefits include sickness pay in addition to a good superannuation scheme. Apply in writing to the address indicated above.

Margin release

If you have to complete a word which cannot be divided, the carriage can be unlocked by pressing the margin-release key (usually found at the top right-hand side of the keyboard). The word can then be completed. Use the margin-release key only when absolutely necessary—a good typist rarely uses it.

Practise margin release

2. Type each of the following sentences exactly as they appear, once for practice and then once for accuracy, using the margin-release where necessary. Use A5 landscape paper (210 × 148 mm) and double-line spacing. Margins: Elite 22–82, Pica 12–72.

A roaring gale had been raging for some days almost incessantly.

She found it extremely difficult to do the job to her satisfaction.

Typing errors should always be neatly rubbed out and corrected.

UNIT 32

Statement of account

Organisations send out at regular intervals (usually monthly), to each of their customers, a Statement of Account showing the balance brought forward (if any) from the previous month; the date and amount of:
(a) invoices sent; (b) credit notes sent; (c) payments received.
It is different from an invoice in that it is a *summary* of a month's transactions, whereas an invoice gives *details* of individual purchases.

Practise typing Statement of Account

1. Study the following Statement of Account. If you do not have a suitable form, place a sheet of A4 paper over the statement below, and lightly trace with pencil the printed ruling. Insert the paper in your typewriter and set margin and tab stops for the start of each column. Then type the statement.

STATEMENT

THE UNIVERSAL SUPPLY CO. LTD.
84—114 High Street
ABERDEEN   AB2 3HE

28th February, 1977

Messrs. J. H. Bowkett & Co.,
25 Crescent Road,
MACDUFF, Banffshire.   AB4 1YA

Fo. 55   Terms: Nett 30 days

Date	Ref.		Debit	Credit	Balance
1977					
Jan. 31		Balance			984.25
Feb. 2	1654	Goods	645.00		1629.25
10	1978	Goods	693.47		2322.72
10		Cheque		984.25	1338.47
15	C.782	Returns		75.00	1263.47
23	2015	Goods	466.38		1729.75

Note: Invoices, Credit Notes, and Statements of Account may or may not have a dividing line between pounds and pence. If there is no dividing line, use the decimal point.

For further exercises on Statements of Account see pages 50 and 62 of **Practical Typing Exercises, Book One**

Guide for line-end division of words

Divide words—

(a) According to syllables
   cur-tain, per-fect
(b) After prefix or before suffix
   com-bine, wait-ing
(c) When consonant is doubled, divide between the two consonants
   excel-lent, neces-sary
(d) Compound words and words already hyphenated must be divided at the hyphen
   pre-eminent, self-taught
(e) The pronunciation of a word must not be changed
   prop-erty *not* pro-perty

Do not divide—

(f) Words of one syllable or their plurals
   niece, nieces; case, cases
(g) At a point which would bring two letters only to the second line
   waited *not* wait-ed
(h) After an initial one-letter syllable
   again *not* a-gain
(i) Proper names
   Johnson, Cambridge
(j) Abbreviations
   C.O.D.   U.S.A.
(k) Numbers or courtesy titles from the word to which they refer
   10 years   Mr. Jones
(l) Sums of money £106.50
(m) On more than 2 consecutive lines

Practise line-end division of words

1. Copy each of the following lines once for practice and then once for accuracy, using A5 landscape paper (210 × 148 mm). Margins: Elite 22–82, Pica 12–72. Note where the word is divided and where division is not possible.

```
sten-cil, pad-lock, mur-mur, pen-cil, prac-tise, elec-trical
com-ply, con-sent, dis-agree, sec-tion, trust-ing, pay-ments
cab-bage, stut-ter, neces-sity, suf-fix, sup-pose, sup-plied
self-support, re-entrance, dinner-time; chil-dren, prob-lems
case, cases, box, boxes, dose, doses; quickly, wrecked, into
unit, await, adore, eject, ideal, obey; Adams, London, Paris
```

2. Type the following paragraph, making correct line-end division where necessary. Use A5 landscape paper (210 × 148 mm) and double spacing. Indent 5 spaces. Set margins at Elite 22–82, Pica 12–72.

Note: The words to be divided are: subsequent, improvement, offset.

```
    This year there was a reduced profit from fire and subsequent
fall in dividends. Motor insurance rates are still too fine, but
it is possible there may be a slight improvement due to the effects
of the energy crisis. Increases in the rates of insurance will be
necessary so that we may offset erosion by inflation.
```

A further exercise in Line-End Division is given on page 12 of **Practical Typing Exercises, Book One**

Skill building

In exercises A and B, type each line or sentence three times. If time permits complete your practice by typing each group of lines as it appears. Keep your eyes on the copy and return the carriage sharply.

Margins:
Elite 22—82
Pica 12—72

A.   Review alphabet keys

1.   After much coaxing, the queer-looking animal eventually was persuaded to jump over the wire on to the trapeze bars.

B.   Increase speed on common word drill

2. arrive please Friday when send will last one you at by of in

3. I hope you will be able to meet us when we arrive next week.

4. Since our short visit last year, we have all been very busy.

| Accuracy practice | 30 w.p.m.   4½ minutes | Not more than four errors |

A.53   I am very pleased to see that a party from your school   11
visited the Moated Tudor Manor House last year, and I hope   23
that the tour was enjoyed by all. From the enclosed Annual   35
Report you will realise that the restoration work could not   47
have been carried out without your help: thank you very much   59
for your donation.   62

     Once again I appeal to you to organize a party from your   73
school. Light refreshments are on sale for the pupils, and   85
the Curator can provide a good "Schoolroom Tea" of tea, sand- 97
wiches, bread and butter, home-made jam, and home-made cakes   109
at 10p a head. If you require any further information,   120
please write direct to the Curator, Mr. E. McGuire, at the   132
above address. (S.I. 1.36)   135

      1 | 2 | 3 | 4 | 5 | 6 | 7 | 8 | 9 | 10 | 11 | 12 |

| Speed building | 40 w.p.m.   1½ minutes | Not more than three errors |

S.9   It is a clear May evening. The shadows of the trees on   11
the fields become long as the sun sinks in the west, and the   23
sky is tinged with red, pink, and gold. We are told that   34
this type of sunset means a fine day tomorrow, and we hope   46
this is true. Now the sun has sunk, and the red glow remains 58
for a time. (S.I. 1.13)   60

S.10   We hear that you are planning to buy some new office   10
desks, and we enclose one of our books on this subject. We   22
feel sure that the points we raise about making good use of   34
the space you have will be of much interest to you. Choose   46
the desks and chairs you would like, and we will advise you   58
on a scheme. (S.I. 1.15)   60

      1 | 2 | 3 | 4 | 5 | 6 | 7 | 8 | 9 | 10 | 11 | 12 |

Record your progress—page 130

UNIT 83

127

Skill building

In exercises A, B and C, type each line or sentence three times. If time permits, complete your practice by typing each group of lines as it appears. Keep your eyes on the copy and return the carriage sharply.

Margins:
Elite 22—82
Pica 12—72

A. Review alphabet keys

1. Faith quickly jumped over the burning boxes, and walked away from the scene of the disaster with dazed feelings.

Practise F to R to 5 back to F

B. Practise 5 and £ key—F finger

2. fr5f fr5f f5rf f5rf 5 firs 5 fees 55 feet 55 files 55 fires.

3. We sold 5 pairs size 5 shoes to 5 men and 5 girls in 5 days.

ONE space before £ but NO space after

Depress right shift key for £

4. fr£f fr£f f£rf f£rf £5, £55, £54, £53, £52, £57, £58 and £59

5. Buy 5 @ £5, 5 @ £4, 5 @ £54, 85 @ £45, 58 @ £55 and 59 @ £55

Practise J to Y to 6 back to J

C. Practise 6 and _ (underscore) key—J finger

6. jy6j jy6j j6yj j6yj 6 jars 6 jugs 66 jobs 66 jets 66 jewels.

7. Bring 6 bags, 6 toys, 6 rods, 6 pots, 6 hoes, also 6 sticks.

Depress left shift key for underscore

8. ju_j ju_j j_uj j_uj jy6j j6yj j6yj jy6j jy6j £56, £65, 1976.

Before underscoring, back-space by depressing the back-space key. After underscoring, always tap space bar. Do NOT underscore final punctuation.

9. Send only 2. See me today. Ask again. Do reply by return.

Note: In Accuracy/Speed Practice and Record Your Progress exercises, pay particular attention to words that have been divided at line-ends.

Accuracy/speed practice   26 w.p.m.   One minute   Not more than one error

A/S.18   Please tell them that there is no need to send a cheque   11
until the goods are sent. If it is their wish, then we will   23
sell on credit. (S.I. 1.08)   26

A/S.19   The guests could not leave till the storm was over, but   11
in spite of the rain all of us thought it had been an excel-   23
lent evening. (S.I. 1.19)   26

1 | 2 | 3 | 4 | 5 | 6 | 7 | 8 | 9 | 10 | 11 | 12 |

Record your progress   One minute

R.9   Once a month a firm will send to its customers a state-   11
ment of account which shows how much they owe to the firm at   23
the end of a month. It will also list the goods bought dur-   35
ing a month. (S.I. 1.16)   38

1 | 2 | 3 | 4 | 5 | 6 | 7 | 8 | 9 | 10 | 11 | 12 |

2. On a suitable form type the following credit note.

CREDIT NOTE   No. C.790

THE UNIVERSAL SUPPLY CO. LTD.
84–114 High Street
ABERDEEN   AB2 3HE

VAT Reg. No. 992 3872 78   17th February, 1977

Messrs. F. J. Barker & Sons,
31 Queen's Road,
FRASERBURGH, Aberdeenshire.   AB4 5PQ

Reason for credit	Quantity and description	Total credit excluding VAT	VAT credited	
			Rate	Amount
		£	%	£
Delivery charged in error	Delivery charge	1.25	25	0.31
	Total Credit	1.25		0.31
	Total VAT	0.31		
	Total amount credited	£1.56		

Original tax invoice no. 1733
dated 3rd February, 1977

3. On a suitable form type the following credit note from the The Universal Supply Co. Ltd. (address as above). No. C.883 dated 24th February, 1977.

To: T. R. Chisholm & Co. Ltd., 71 Inverness Road, Perth. PH2 8LT

Reason for Credit: Damaged goods

Quantity and description: 1 12" Portable TV Set

Total credit (excluding VAT) £76

VAT Rate: 25% VAT amount: £19

Total credit: £76 Total VAT: £19

Total amount credited: £95

Original tax invoice No. 2007 dated 11th February, 1977

Further exercises on credit notes are given on page 47 of **Practical Typing Exercises, Book One**

Technique development

Effective display

Important lines can be given prominence by using:

(a) Spaced capitals, i.e., leave *one space between letters* and *3 spaces between words*.
(b) Closed capitals, i.e., leave NO space between letters and ONE space between words.
(c) Capitals and small letters.
(d) Underscoring. (Do not underscore punctuation mark at end of lines).

Practise making your display effective

1. Display the following notice on A5 landscape paper (210 × 148 mm). Notice the use of spaced capitals, closed capitals, and underscore to stress important lines. Centre vertically and horizontally.

A N N U A L   D I N N E R

will be held

<u>on 31st January, 1977</u>

at the

<u>GRAND HOTEL</u>

Reception 7 p.m.

Tickets obtainable from the

SOCIAL CLUB SECRETARY

NOTE: Leave ONE space between 7 and p; NO space after . following p

2. Display the following notice on A5 portrait paper (148 × 210 mm), making it as effective as possible. Centre vertically and horizontally.

Fashion Show Preview to be held in the Norfolk

Room at 10 a.m. on 22nd and 23rd March.

Open to trade only. Tickets obtainable by

application to Sales Manager.

Hadfield (Warehouses) Ltd., Great North Street,

Huddersfield. HD2 1XU

Further display exercises are given on pages 1, 2, 3, 12 and 20 of **Practical Typing Exercises, Book One**

Credit Notes

(a) Usually printed and typed in red.
(b) Used to cancel an incorrect invoice. (A new, correct, invoice would then be issued.)
(c) Used for crediting goods or packing cases returned.
(d) A supplier who credits a customer for goods/services relating to taxable supplies must issue a VAT credit note which should give: VAT registration no., amount credited for each item, rate and amount of VAT credited, etc. (For full details of VAT Regulations as applied to credit notes, please see **Practical Typing Exercises, Book One**, page 46.)

Practise typing credit notes

1. Type the following credit note on a suitable form. If you do not have a printed credit note form, place a sheet of A4 paper over the credit note below, and lightly trace with a pencil the printed ruling.

CREDIT NOTE   No. C.782

THE UNIVERSAL SUPPLY CO. LTD.
84-114 High Street
ABERDEEN   AB2 3HE

VAT Reg. No. 992 3872 78   15th February, 1977

Messrs. J. H. Bowkett & Co.,
25 Crescent Road,
MACDUFF, Banffshire.   AB4 1YA

Reason for credit	Quantity and description	Total credit excluding VAT	VAT credited	
			Rate	Amount
		£	%	£
Returned goods (damaged)	1 Single Lens Camera	60.00	25	15.00
	Total credit	60.00		15.00
	Total VAT	15.00		
	Total amount credited	£75.00		

Original tax invoice No. 1654
dated 2nd February, 1977

Consolidation

Margins: Elite 27—77
Pica 18—68

A. Alphabet keys

1.   Extra large quantities of iced jellies, cakes and wines have to be prepared by the young members of that excellent organization.

B. Figures

2. we 23 24 25 you 697 678 789 rut 475 456 567 to 69.

3. Read pages 23, 24, and 45.   Check pages 67 and 90.

4. 23rd March, 1978; 4th April, 1960; 6th July, 1976.

5. Please ring 021-345 6780 at 1345 on 19th February.

C. Special characters

6. "2" 3/3 4 @ £5 <u>6</u> 7 & 7 '8' (9) (10) "27 & 72" 2-3.

7. He said, "Will the FULL-TIME SCORE be read later?"

8. We/They require 2 (two) @ £10 each - <u>not 22</u> @ £10.

9. 'To be or not to be' is from Shakespeare's HAMLET.

Note use of ' for single quotes

D. Shift key

10. Dear, Yours, Sir, Mr., New York, Hong Kong, James.

11. Dear Sir, Dear Mr., Yours truly, Yours faithfully.

12. Hamburg-America Line, 109 Jermyn Street, New York.

13. We do not want every Tom, Dick and Harry to apply.

E. Punctuation

Reminder: TWO spaces after full stop and question mark at end of sentence.
ONE space after comma, colon and semi-colon.
ONE space before and after dash.
NO space before or after hyphen.
NO space before or after apostrophe when it comes *before* the *s*.

14. "Is this Ann's dog?" "Yes it is.   Leave it here."

15. Please order: 2 brown, 3 black, 4 red, and 5 blue.

16. Mary hurried; so did I - we were indeed very late.

17. May I have an up-to-date calendar? I will get it.

2. On a suitable form type the following invoice.

INVOICE   No. 1733

THE UNIVERSAL SUPPLY CO. LTD.
84–114 High Street
ABERDEEN AB2 3HE

VAT Registration No. 992 3872 78   Date: 3rd February, 1977

Messrs. F. J. Barker & Sons,
31 Queen's Road,
FRASERBURGH, Aberdeenshire. AB4 5PQ

Your Order No. 975/77   Terms: Nett 30 days

Tax Point	Type of Supply	Description	Quantity	Price	VAT Rate	VAT Amount
				£	%	£
3.2.77	Sale	8-digit Calculators 4 Functions @ £25 ea.	4	100.00	25	25.00
3.2.77	Sale	8-digit Calculators 4 Functions, 1 memory @ £40 ea.	5	200.00	25	50.00
				300.00		75.00
		Delivery charge (Nett)		1.25	25	0.31
		Total goods		301.25		75.31
		Total VAT (Nett)		75.31		
		Total amount due		£376.56		

Further exercises on invoices are given on pages 44 and 45 of **Practical Typing Exercises, Book One**

Record your progress   Four minutes

R.26   We were very glad to learn from your letter of 16th July   11
that the prospects you spoke of when you called on us 3 weeks   23
ago are now materialising.   28

        You tell us that you have bought a new truck for busi-   39
ness and that you are able to save storage charges by hous-   51
ing it in your own factory building. We are sure that you   62
have calculated well and that the truck will cut down your   73
expenses.   75

        Have you had your insurance broker review your insur-   86
ance? We venture to suggest that you go over your policy   98
with your broker to ensure that there are no mistakes in it.   110
The fact that you have this truck in your works will change   122
the rates and may invalidate the policy. (S.I. 1.33)   130

  1 | 2 | 3 | 4 | 5 | 6 | 7 | 8 | 9 | 10 | 11 | 12 |

Books of reference

The efficient typist or secretary carries in her head only essential information that she uses frequently. She knows immediately where to check or find unusual or important information. She makes constant use of good reference books. Here is a short list of some books that you will find useful:

1. Standard Dictionary
2. Post Office Guide
3. Street Directory
4. Roget's *Thesaurus of English Words and Phrases*
5. Telephone Directory
6. A.A. Handbook
7. Handbook for Typists and Secretaries

Can you suggest one reason for using each of the above books? (See Page 151 for answers)

Review Quiz No. 1

To speed up your production typing, you must be able quickly to apply important details such as spacing after punctuation, correct use of hyphen, dash, and so on. The following is a Review Quiz for you to complete. Type the following sentences, filling in the words needed to give the correct answer. Do not write on your textbook.

1. Leave . . . space after comma, semicolon, and colon.
2. Leave . . . spaces after full stop at end of sentence.
3. Leave . . . spaces after question mark at end of sentence.
4. Leave . . . space/s before and after hyphen.
5. Leave . . . spaces for first word of indented paragraph.
6. Leave . . . space/s before or after apostrophe in the middle of a word.
7. Leave . . . space before but . . . spaces after quotation mark at the end of a sentence.
8. At the end of a lesson you should always . . . your typewriter.
9. Leave . . . space/s before and after dash.
10. Feet should be . . . on the floor; back . . . ; arms and wrists . . .
11. There are . . . pica spaces and . . . elite spaces in full width of A4 paper.
12. There are . . . single-line spaces on a sheet of A4 paper and . . . single-line spaces on a sheet of A5 landscape paper (210 × 148 mm) and on A5 portrait paper (148 × 210 mm) . . . single-line spaces.
13. Leave . . . space after £ sign.
14. Do . . . underscore final punctuation mark.
15. Capital letters require use of . . . key.
16. Leave . . . space/s before and after ampersand.
17. Leave . . . space/s before and after solidus.
18. 210 × 297 mm is . . . paper; 148 × 210 mm is . . . . . . paper and 210 × 148 mm is . . . . . . paper.
19. When typing a word in all capitals, depress the . . . . . .
20. Divide compound words and words already hyphenated at the . . .
21. Do . . . divide at a point which would bring . . . letters to second line.
22. Words of one syllable must . . . be divided.
23. Do . . . divide words on more than . . . consecutive lines.
24. Do not divide . . . or . . . names.
25. Numbers or courtesy titles should . . . be separated from the word to which they refer.

Turn to page 151 and check your answers. Score one point for each correct entry.
Total score—39

Technique development

Invoices

An invoice is the document sent by the seller to the purchaser and shows full details of the goods sold. The layout of invoices varies from firm to firm according to the information to be given. Invoices are always printed with the seller's name, address, and other useful information.

A trader registered for VAT who supplies taxable goods to another taxable person must issue a VAT invoice giving the VAT registration number, tax point, type of supply, etc. (For full details of VAT Regulations as applied to invoices, please see **Practical Typing Exercises, Book One**, page 43.)

Practise typing invoices

1. If you do not have a suitable invoice form, place a sheet of A4 paper over the exercise below, and lightly trace with a pencil the printed ruling. Insert the paper in your typewriter and set margin and tab stops for the beginning of each column. Then type the invoice exactly as it appears.

INVOICE   No. 1654

THE UNIVERSAL SUPPLY CO. LTD.
84-114 High Street
ABERDEEN   AB2 3HE

VAT Registration No. 992 3872 78   Date: 2nd February, 1977

Messrs. J. H. Bowkett & Co.,
25 Crescent Road,
MACDUFF, Banffshire.   AB4 1YA

Your Order No. PUR 972/77   Terms: Nett 30 days

Tax Point	Type of Supply	Description	Quantity	Price	VAT Rate	VAT Amount
				£	%	£
2. 2. 77	Sale	Single Lens Reflex Cameras @ £60 ea.	5	300.00	25	75.00
2. 2. 77	Sale	Cine Cameras — 9–30 mm Zoom @ £108 ea.	2	216.00	25	54.00
		Total Goods		516.00		129.00
		Total VAT (Nett)		129.00		
		Total amount due		£645.00		
E & O E						

In exercises A, B and C, type each line or sentence three times. If time permits, complete your practice by typing each group of lines as it appears. Keep your eyes on the copy and return the carriage sharply.

A. Review alphabet keys

Margins:
Elite 22—82
Pica 12—72

1. The exhausted travellers, frozen by the cruel wind, and dazed and weary from lack of rest, joined hands and squeezed their way past the gaping chasm to safety.

B. Build speed on fluency drills

2. Did for the key all dog why see you put car ask new her site

3. She did not see the new bus. Ask her for all the old shoes.

4. Tom has won the new car. Buy all the tea you can. See May.

5. Put out the cat and the dog now. You may see him for a day.

C. Build speed on phrase drills

6. to me, to go, to ask, to see, to get, to the, to her, to him

7. I am to ask you to see if you can go to the game on Tuesday.

8. I will talk to him as soon as he is ready to go to the play.

9. In order to get to them, you must come to me for a road map.

Accuracy/speed practice	26 w.p.m. 1½ minutes	Not more than two errors

A/S.20   We feel we must write to say how sorry we were to learn   11
that the men in your works have come out on strike over what   23
is just a small dispute. We do trust that they will soon be   35
back at work again. (S.I. 1.10)   39

A/S.21   As a typist you must be fast, accurate, and able to set   11
out all kinds of documents. In your first post there may be   23
some forms of layout that are not clear, and, if that is so,   35
you should seek help. (S.I. 1.18)   39

1 | 2 | 3 | 4 | 5 | 6 | 7 | 8 | 9 | 10 | 11 | 12 |

Record your progress   1½ minutes

R.10   Some months have passed since you left the Sales Office   11
to study accounts, and we feel it is now a good time to dis-   23
cuss your future. In the past 10 years we have been pleased   35
with the high standard of your work and are sure you will do   47
well in the future. (S.I. 1.14)   51

1 | 2 | 3 | 4 | 5 | 6 | 7 | 8 | 9 | 10 | 11 | 12 |

Skill building

Type exercises A, B and C three times. Keep your eyes on the copy and return the carriage sharply.

A.   Review alphabet keys

1.   I expected to make just sufficient space for the quaint old table with the green baize top by removing the armchair.

B.   Build accuracy on letter-combinations

2. additional committee entitled definite credits remits visits

3. transport effort report inform story order work word for ore

4. Your committee are entitled to free transport for the visit.

5. Make a definite effort to prepare an additional credit note.

C.   Improve accuracy on word-building drill

6. tend attend attends attended attending attendance attendants

7. be belie belief believe believes believed believing believer

8. We believe their attendance has tended to be poor this term.

9. The attendants believe that the attendance will now improve.

Accuracy practice   30 w.p.m.   Four minutes   Not more than four errors

A.52   Please note that as from 22nd December there will be an   11
increase of 25 per cent in air fares because of higher land-   23
ing charges.   25

      You are reminded that you must comply with police and   36
customs regulations at the points of departure and arrival,   48
and along the route. A journey may be broken at most stops   60
with no extra charge, on condition that you complete the   72
journey within the dates stated. As there are a number of   84
formalities to be complied with, the "check-in" time quoted   96
on your ticket is the time by which you must present your-   108
self with your luggage - if you are late, you will miss the   119
plane. (S.I. 1.33)   120

      1 | 2 | 3 | 4 | 5 | 6 | 7 | 8 | 9 | 10 | 11 | 12 |

Speed building   40 w.p.m.   One minute   Not more than two errors

S.7   Thank you for your note just to hand. We have received   11
the rest of our last order, and now enclose a cheque for the   23
full amount due. We shall be glad if you will keep in touch   35
with us from time to time. (S.I. 1.10)   40

S.8   The bright sunshine brought out more cars, thus causing   11
traffic in the narrow streets to be slowed down to a snail's   23
pace. To walk was the one sure way of getting from place to   35
place in the shortest time. (S.I. 1.15)   40

      1 | 2 | 3 | 4 | 5 | 6 | 7 | 8 | 9 | 10 | 11 | 12 |

Record your progress —page 124

Technique development

Paragraphing

Paragraphs are used to separate the different subjects or sections. This breaks the writing into short passages to facilitate reading and understanding. There are three different forms of paragraphing, viz., blocked, indented and hanging.

Practise using blocked paragraphs

1. Type the following on A5 landscape paper (210 × 148 mm), using blocked paragraphs as shown. Margins; Elite 22–82, Pica 12–72.

As you have already learnt, in blocked paragraphs all lines start at the same scale-point.

This form is normally used in single-line typing, in which case you turn up 2 single-line spaces between the paragraphs, as in this exercise.

When double-line spacing, however, is used, you should turn up 3 single-line spaces between the paragraphs.

Indented paragraphs

As you have learnt when typing Accuracy and Speed Practice exercises, the first line of each paragraph is indented. This indentation is made by setting a tab stop five spaces from the point fixed for the left margin. When using indented paragraphs, two single-line spaces only should be turned up between the paragraphs, whether single or double-line spacing is used.

Hanging paragraphs

Practise using hanging paragraphs

2. Type the following in single-line spacing on A5 landscape paper (210 × 148 mm), using hanging paragraphs as shown and margins Elite 22–82, Pica 12–72.

A third type of paragraph is known as a hanging paragraph. This means that the first line of the paragraph starts 2 spaces to the left of the second and subsequent lines, as in this exercise.

Hanging paragraphs are sometimes used in display work and in certain documents, such as building specifications.

Leave your desk tidy

(a) Using paper release lever, draw out paper, and return the lever to the normal position.
(b) Place paper bail against cylinder.
(c) Centre carriage by holding the right cylinder knob, pressing carriage release and moving carriage to middle. Release carriage release.
(d) Always cover your typewriter and put your papers away tidily.

Typing postcards and memoranda

When typing postcards or memoranda you may have, of necessity, to type near the bottom of the paper. To ensure that your typewriter grips the paper and thus prevents the bottom line from 'running off' the paper, always use a backing sheet.

Review Quiz No. 5

1. When typing sums of money in columns, . . . figures must appear in the pence after the decimal point.

2. The £ sign should be centred over the . . . figure of the pounds.

3. To type double lines underneath totals, use the . . .

4. After typing the double line, . . . the . . . lever to its normal position.

5. The underscore line should not extend . . . or . . . the £ sign.

6. A boxed table has . . . lines between the columns.

7. The vertical lines should be ruled precisely in the . . . of each blank space between the columns.

8. After typing the final horizontal line at the bottom of a table, mark the . . . of the vertical lines in pencil.

9. Do not allow vertical lines to extend . . . or . . . the horizontal lines.

10. In ruled tables the left and right sides may be closed by . . . . . .

11. It is advisable to leave . . . or . . . spaces between columns of a table.

12. A message from one department to another takes the form of a . . .

13. The variable line-spacer is on the . . . cylinder knob. It is used to move the . . . . . . to any desired position.

14. When typing details on dotted or ruled lines or completing a form letter, the . . . . . . should be used.

15. Wording to be typed on dotted or ruled lines should be slightly . . . the lines so that no portion of a character appears . . . the lines.

16. In an inter-office memorandum there is no . . . and no . . . . . .

17. Always leave . . . . . . spaces before typing after printed words in memoranda or form letters.

18. To indicate an enclosure type the abbreviation . . . or . . . if more than one at the . . . margin.

19. To fill in wording in a form letter, insert the form letter into the machine so that the first line of the body of the letter is just . . . the . . . . . .

20. When writing to individuals always insert a . . . . . .

21. In work other than display and tabulations the . . . margin should be slightly wider than the . . . . . .

Turn to page 151 and check your answers. Score one point for each correct entry.
Total score: 40

Types of display headings

Headings are typed in different ways. The main heading, i.e., the title of a passage, may be blocked or centred on the typing line. It may be typed in closed or spaced capitals. If spaced capitals are used, one space is left between each letter and three spaces between each word. If in closed capitals, no space is left between letters and one space is left between words. The sub-heading is also blocked or centred on the typing line and is separated from the main heading by one blank line, i.e., turn up two single-line spaces after the main heading. After the sub-heading, turn up three single-line spaces. To centre headings on typing line when margins are unequal, find the centre point of the typing line by adding together the two margins and dividing by 2. Examples:

Margins set at Elite 22–82: 22 + 82
= 104 ÷ 2 = 52 centre point
Pica 12–72: 12 + 72
= 84 ÷ 2 = 42 centre point

Practise typing main and sub-headings

1. Type a copy of the following on A5 landscape paper (210 × 148 mm), using blocked paragraphs and single spacing. Centre the main heading and the sub-heading. Margins: Elite 22–82, Pica 12–72.

TYPES OF DISPLAY HEADINGS

(Turn up 2 single spaces)

Guide for Typists

(Turn up 3 single spaces)

When there is a sub-heading, as in this exercise, it is typed usually in lower-case letters and must be underscored. It is separated from the main heading by one blank line, i.e., turn up two single-line spaces.

After typing the sub-heading, turn up three single-line spaces.

Paragraph headings

Apart from main headings and sub-headings, paragraph headings are used to indicate sub-divisions under the main heading. In blocked style, the heading starts at the left margin as in Exercise 2 below; if indented style is used, the heading starts at the paragraph indentation.

Practise typing paragraph headings

2. Type a copy of the following on A5 landscape paper (210 × 148 mm), using margins Elite 22–82, Pica 12–72. Centre the main heading, using spaced capitals; for sub-heading use lower case with initial capitals for each word and underscore.

G U I D E   T O   T Y P I S T S

Paragraph Headings

Paragraph headings: These may be typed with initial capital and lower case letters and underscored or in closed capitals with or without the underscore. The paragraph heading may be followed by a punctuation mark (the normal spacing being used after the punctuation mark) as in this paragraph.

Paragraph headings may run on without punctuation as in this paragraph and, if typed in lower case, must be underscored.

Further exercises on Paragraph Headings are given on Page 26 of **Practical Typing Exercises, Book One**

(a) Type the following exercises on A5 portrait paper. Use margins of Elite 12–62, Pica 5–55, and take a carbon copy. Use double spacing.

Note: There is ALWAYS a clear space between (a) the last typed character and the beginning of the dots, (b) the last dot and the next typed character.

ENROLMENT FORM

Surname ....

Christian name(s) ....

Address ....

....

Age .... Date of birth ....

Qualifications ....

....

....

Course Code ....

Aim of Course ....

(b) On the carbon copy complete the form with your own name, address and other details required.

Record your progress   3½ minutes

R.25   Today it is a very common thing to meet a person for   10
the first time over the telephone. It is not unusual for   21
2 people to have talked to each other many times over the   33
telephone without meeting. What kind of person are you when   45
you talk over the phone? Do you speak clearly? Have you a   56
'voice with a smile'?   60

       The good secretary deals with phone calls promptly and   71
efficiently. She is aware that first impressions are impor-   83
tant, and so makes the caller feel that an interest is being   95
taken and that she is anxious to help. Courtesy and tact   107
are second nature to her and gain her many friends. **(S.I. 1.36)** 117

     1 | 2 | 3 | 4 | 5 | 6 | 7 | 8 | 9 | 10 | 11 | 12 |

Shoulder headings

When this form of heading is used, it is typed in closed capitals at the left margin and usually underscored, and is preceded and followed by one blank line as in the exercise below.

Practise typing shoulder headings

1. Type a copy of the following on A5 landscape paper (210 × 148 mm), using block paragraphs and single-line spacing, and set margins at Elite 22–82, Pica 12–72. Centre the main heading on the typing line.

<u>CARE OF THE TYPEWRITER</u>
(Turn up 3 single-line spaces)

<u>DAILY</u>
(Turn up 2 single-line spaces)

Clean the type faces of your machine with a stiff brush, and dust the inside carefully with a long-handled brush. Remove all dust from underneath the machine. Always cover your typewriter when not in use.
(Turn up 2 single-line spaces)

<u>WEEKLY</u>
(Turn up 2 single-line spaces)

Dampen a soft cloth with oil and wipe the carriage rails. Do not oil any other parts.

<u>ERASING</u>
(Turn up 2 single-line spaces)

Always move carriage to extreme left or right to prevent rubber dust from falling into the mechanism of the machine.

Side headings

These headings are typed inside the left margin and usually in closed capitals with or without underscore. They are used particularly in specifications and similar documents, characters in plays, etc. The following steps should be taken:

(a) First decide on left and right margins.
(b) Set right margin.
(c) Where you intended to set left margin, set a tab stop.
(d) Tap in once for each character and space in the longest line of side headings plus 3 extra spaces.
(e) At this point set left margin.
(f) To type side headings, use margin release, bringing typing point to tab stop set in (c).

Practise typing side headings

2. Type the following on A5 landscape paper (210 × 148 mm), using block paragraphs, single-line spacing and side headings. Margins: Elite 22–82, Pica 12–72.

EXTRACT FROM MINUTES OF BOARD MEETING
HELD ON 27TH AUGUST 1977

Set margin at Elite 37 Pica 27

Set tab stop at OVERTIME   It was unanimously agreed that overtime pay-
Elite 22 Pica 12   ment should be made in accordance with in-
                           structions given in the Union Circular No. 28.

LONG SERVICE   Agreed that a cheque for £100 should be given
                to each of the 4 employees who had been in the
                Company's employment for 40 years.

Further exercises on Shoulder Headings and Side Headings are given on pages 26 and 27 of **Practical Typing Exercises, Book One**

Type the following on A4 paper, using paragraph headings. Choose suitable margins and use hanging paragraphs.

OFFSET LITHOGRAPHY

l.c. Preparation of Master. You can type, write or draw on the
27/uch plate; guide lines may be drawn on the master
w a water-colour or pencil. non-reproducing

Making corrections. Pencil or typewritten errors can
be corrected w a soft eraser or correcting fluid.
With an eraser, care shd be taken to avoid
damaging the surface of the plate.

H Photo copying process. An original may be photo-
copied on to a master.

H Proof reading. It is absolutely essential, as a great
no. of copies is likely to be produced, th the
l.c. Master plate is thoroughly checked before being
run off. Proof-reading is most effective when it is
done:
(a) By 2 persons – one reading to the other;
(b) by someone other than the person who typed
the master. original

Job 26

Display the following table on A5 portrait paper and rule. Use double spacing for the body, and type in centred or block style.

TYPISTS

1977 SALARY SCALES

	Scale	Maximum	Minimum
	1	£1,144	£1,040
trs.	2	£1,552	£1,248
	3	£1,560	£1,664 1,456
	4	£1,768	£1,664
trs	5	£2,284	£2,180
	6	£2,076	£1,872

Skill building

Type each exercise (A, B and C) three times. Keep your eyes on the copy and return the carriage sharply.

Margins:
Elite 22—82
Pica 12—72

A.   Review alphabet keys

1.   The liquid is just what is needed; but I must criticize
the price asked and the most waxy finish which it now gives.

B.   Practise line-end division

2. go-ing, com-ing, ask-ing, say-ing, pay-ing, mak-ing, aim-ing

3. use-less, wit-less, aim-less, end-less, help-less, hope-less

4. sub-mit, sub-let, sub-way, sub-tract, sub-stance, sub-scribe

5. com-bine, com-pact, com-mend, com-mand, com-pare, com-pleted

C.   Build accuracy on one-hand words

6. fed join daze kill safe look arts hill gate pony trees imply

7. upon raft only ebbs yolk wave mill bear null vase loop caves

8. See them feed that pony by the gate near the old water mill.

9. The raft in the caves looked as if the waves had smashed it.

Accuracy/speed practice   26 w.p.m.   Two minutes   Not more than two errors

A/S.22   Last May our buyer had a chance to buy a large stock of   11
fine nylon sheets - 950 pairs - and we are now selling these   23
at a reduced price. If your own stock of sheets is low, now   35
is a chance to buy these items at half price. Send an order   47
within the next 10 days. (S.I. 1.13)   52

A/S.23   I hope to come and see you soon, but I fear it will not   11
be until the end of June, as at the moment we are so busy at   23
the office that I feel it would not be wise for me to leave.   35
Next week I have to go away, but I feel sure it will be pos-   47
sible to visit you soon. (S.I. 1.15)   52

    1 | 2 | 3 | 4 | 5 | 6 | 7 | 8 | 9 | 10 | 11 | 12 |

Record your progress   Two minutes

R.11   On sheet one we set out the pay scales agreed to at the   11
last meeting. You will see that salaries above point 72 are   23
to be increased by £155 a year, and scales from 72 and below   35
will rise by £360 a year. May we ask you to tell your staff   47
about this award on Thursday next. The new rates are effec-   59
tive as from March 1977. (S.I. 1.19)   64

    1 | 2 | 3 | 4 | 5 | 6 | 7 | 8 | 9 | 10 | 11 | 12 |

Type an original and two carbon copies of the following letter. Use suitable margins and mark the letter for the attention of George T. Hamilton. In the top left-hand corner of the first carbon copy type the following: MR. L. MATTHEWS – FOR INFORMATION.

Our Ref. FJA/ME   Today's date
J. Barker & Sons, 74 Thomas Street, Liverpool.   L6 5BJ

Dear Sirs, We obtained your address from the enclosed advertisement which appeared in OFFICE SUPPLIES.
Would you please quote us for the following Teak Unit Furniture:

UF 477   Sliding Door Unit   500 × 700 × 400 mm
UF 833   4-drawer Unit   500 × 500 × 400 mm
UF 983   Open Storage Unit   500 × 500 × 245 mm

In the first instance we would place an order for 3 of each item, but, should this type of furniture prove popular, we would then order in larger quantities. Please let us know your Trade and Cash Discount Terms.

Yours faithfully, Midland Furniture Co. Ltd., F. J. Adams, Purchasing Officer.

Job 23   Production Target—six minutes

Display the following notice on A5 portrait paper. Centre the whole notice vertically. The longest line should be centred horizontally and all lines blocked at the same scale-point as the longest line.

Ye Olde Moat House Club (caps)
Gosport, Hants.
Telephone: Gosport (code 070 17) 2140
Luncheons + Evening Meals
Suppers Late/License + Dancing Nightly. LICENCE
Special Dance + Cabaret Too Shows every Saturday

Job 24   Production Target—nine minutes

Display the following exercise on A5 landscape paper and rule. Use double spacing for the body, and type in centred or block style.

AGENTS (spaced caps + underscore)

Port	Names	Telegraphic Address
Durban	J. S. Union + Co.	Union, Durban
Boston	Wm. J. George Inc.	Sans, Boston
Melbourne	Lyndon + Co. Ltd.	Luxury, Melbourne
Vancouver	L. G. Davis Inc.	Anchor, Vancouver

Technique development

Typing from manuscript copy

You may have to type letters or documents from hand-written drafts. Take particular care to produce a correct copy and also to fill in any details which may have been omitted, such as dates, names, addresses, etc. Always return the document for examination and signature to the person who drafted it. *Before typing, first read the document through to see that you understand it.* Some words or letters, not very clear in one part, may be repeated in another part more clearly.

Margins:
Elite 22—82
Pica 12—72

Practise typing from manuscript copy

1. Type the following paragraph on A5 landscape paper (210 × 148 mm) in double-line spacing, keeping to the lines as copy. From the top edge of the paper turn up seven single-line spaces. This means that you will leave 25 mm (1 inch) clear at the top. Set tab stop for indent of first line of paragraph. Read the passage through and note where words are divided at the line end.

> We are very pleased to send you a copy of our new catalogue of low-priced furniture. As you will doubtless be aware, costs have been forced up, and we cannot, therefore, maintain our prices for very long. However, if you will forward your order to us before the end of the month, we can still execute it at the prices which we quote in the list.

2. Type the following paragraphs on a sheet of A5 landscape paper (210 × 148 mm) in double-line spacing. From the top edge of the paper turn up seven single-line spaces. Set tab stop for paragraph indents. Read the passage through carefully.
   Note: the words to be divided are: *instruction, exercise, understand, document.*

> It is important that you follow exactly every instruction given about an exercise. At the beginning of the exercise read the instructions and prepare for typing. Then go carefully through the exercise and make sure that you understand it and that it makes sense. If you have a query ask about it before you start to type.
> Typing examiners tell us that you can lose a great many marks if you do not carry out instructions. Also, any document typed for an employer must be typed according to his directions.

Use of eraser

You may find it necessary to make a correction in production typing work. If so, the alteration must be scarcely noticeable. Erase in the following manner, before you take your paper out of the machine.

(a) Turn up paper so that error is on top of the platen or paper table.

(b) Move carriage to extreme left or right to prevent rubber dust from falling into the mechanism of the machine.

(c) Press paper tightly against the platen or paper table to prevent slipping.

(d) Erase the error by rubbing gently up and down, blowing away rubber dust as you do so. (Too much pressure may cause a hole.)

(e) If you are using a new or heavily inked ribbon, erase first with a soft rubber and then with a hard eraser.

(f) Turn paper back to writing line and insert correct letter or letters.

(g) Always use a clean eraser.

Further exercises in manuscript are given on page 19 of **Practical Typing Exercises, Book One**

UNIT 42

Consolidation

Production typing

Job 20

Production Target—twelve minutes

Type the following exercise on A4 paper in single-line spacing. Display the shoulder headings in the usual way. Use margins of Elite 22–82, Pica 12–72, and indented paragraphs.

Miscellaneous Theory   ← Caps & underscore

As a typist in business, or in a typewriting examination, you wl be expected to remember, certain points of theory. Here are a few reminders.

COURTESY TITLES

When writing to individuals, a courtesy title is essential. If you do not know whether a lady is Miss or Mrs., type M/S or Mrs (w/out a full stop). A man shd be addressed as Mr. or Esq., not both. If you use the courtesy title Dr. or Rev., do not use Mr. or Esq. [The word Messrs. is used as a courtesy title for partnerships, e.g., Messrs. Barnes & Son, Messrs. Rodney & Smith.

Margins

It is usual to hv the left margin, wider than the rt margin — except in display work. When using & tabulation A4 paper for business ltrs do not hv a left margin of less than one inch (25 mm), & the rt margin shd not be less than half an inch (13 mm).

Job 21

Production Target—ten minutes

On suitable paper type the following memo, taking a carbon copy. In the top left-hand corner of the carbon copy type the word FILE and underscore it.

From: R. T. Hallett   (Suitable date)
To: Mr. P. Harris   Subject: SALES STATISTICS

In the sales statistics for the last 3 months you give the following comparative figures:

	1976	1977
January	£20,295	£23,176
February	£19,456	£17,982
March	£25,789	£24,765

At the sales meeting on 7th April you said that the 1977 figures for February and March were up on the previous year's figures. Please check the figures quoted above and let me know if they are correct.

Technique development

Longhand abbreviations

In a rough draft of manuscript copy certain longhand words may be abbreviated, but these must be typed in full. The sense of the matter will help you to do this. Some of these abbreviations are given below.

Abbreviation	Word in full	Abbreviation	Word in full
a/c	account	ref	reference
amt	amount	sec	secretary
bn	been	sh	shall
co	company	shd	should
dept	department	th	that
exs	expenses	togr	together
f	for	w	with
fr	from	wd	would
hv	have	wh	which
pd	paid	wl	will
recd	received	yr	your, year
rect	receipt		

Note: & (ampersand), Co., and Ltd., are only abbreviated in the names of companies.

Practise typing from manuscript copy

1. After studying the above abbreviations, read the following passage to see that you understand it, and then type a copy on A5 landscape paper (210 × 148 mm). All abbreviations to be typed in full. Leave 6 clear spaces at the top of the page. Set tab stop for paragraph indent.

> Although conditions hv not bn easy f yr Co during the past 12 mths, y wl see fr the a/cs in yr possession th last yr closed w a slight increase in turnover, wh enables us to submit a favourable report on the year's trading; the present year's prospects are good.

2. Type the following on A5 landscape paper (210 × 148 mm), rendering all abbreviations in full. Leave 6 clear spaces at top of page. Set tab stop for paragraph indent.

> We hv recd yr applicn in reply to our advert in today's POST f a Junior Shtd-Typist. We note th y are 18 yrs of age & th y hv obtd 'O' levels in 6 subjects. We think th y wl be suitable f the vacant posn & shd therefore be pleased to see y on Wed next at 2 p.m. We wd like y to bring w y yr refs togr w any certs wh you hv.

Further exercises in manuscript with longhand abbreviations are given on page 22 of **Practical Typing Exercises, Book One**

UNIT 43

53

4. (a) Prepare the following skeleton letter, taking two carbon copies. Use
   A5 portrait paper and margins of Elite 12–62, Pica 5–55.

J. A. RANKIN & CO. LTD.
Trinity Road,
Luton, Bedfordshire.   LU4 5TJ

(Turn up three single-line spaces)

Our Ref.

(Turn up eleven single-line spaces)

For the attention of
(Turn up 2 single-line spaces)
Dear Sirs,

We thank you for your order dated (leave blank)
and numbered (eight blanks). We have pleasure in advising
you that delivery will be made in (three blanks) weeks.

Yours faithfully,
J. A. RANKIN & CO. LTD.

Manager

(b) Using the original prepared above, insert the following information:

   Our Ref. FE/your initials   Today's date
   Addressee   F. L. Wilkes Ltd., 24–28 High Street, Brierley Hill,
   West Midlands.   DY3 1DE   For the attention of Mr. F. L. Wilkes
   Order dated insert suitable date   and numbered S.2906
   Delivery in 4 weeks.

(c) Using a carbon copy prepared in (a) above, insert the following
   information:

   Our Ref.   FE/your initials   Today's date
   Addressee   T. Chambers & Co. Ltd., 20 Market Street, Huddersfield,
   Yorkshire.   HD1 2NE   For the attention of Mr. W. Franklyn
   order dated   insert suitable date   and numbered   P.3347
   Delivery in 2 weeks.

(d) Using the remaining carbon copy, insert the following information:

   Our Ref.   FE/your initials   Today's date
   Addressee   Jones & King Ltd., Lionel Street, Burton-upon-Trent,
   Staffordshire.   DE13 1NF   For the attention of Mr. L. Yates
   order dated   insert suitable date   and numbered A.6834
   Delivery in 3 weeks.

Further exercises on Form Letters are given on pages 40, 41 and 42 of **Practical Typing Exercises, Book One**

Skill building

In exercises A, B and C, type each line or sentence three times. If time permits, complete your practice by typing each group of lines as it appears. Keep your eyes on the copy and return the carriage sharply.

Margins:
Elite 22—82
Pica 12—72

A.   Review alphabet keys

1.   Judy was thinking of increasing the size of her antique shop, which, she said, would leave enough room for exhibits.

B.   Improve control of space bar

2. a s d f j k l a b c d e f g h i j k l m n o p q r s t u v w.

3. as is so or be in am if an me go my do he by us ask may you.

4. It is so. Ask me to go. You must be in time. I may do so.

5. She can get home. Let me see all the old hats. Who is she?

C.   Build speed on fluency drills

6. with hand they keys when lame them make both half rush paid.

7. also held firm name work owns wish pale form hail down male.

8. Rush with both keys when they hand them down to the two men.

9. The firm will also wish them both to be paid when they call.

Accuracy/speed practice   27 w.p.m.   One minute   Not more than one error

A/S.24   To give our legs a rest, John and I sat down on a stone   11
ledge near the edge of the cliff. Tom thought he would look   23
for wild birds' eggs. (S.I. 1.00)   27

A/S.25   The day was sunny but cool. When we had rested and had   11
a snack we packed our bags and set out for the distant head-   23
land shrouded in mist. (S.I. 1.18)   27

A/S.26   We could hear the waves battering against the rocks be-   11
low and, as we travelled on, the clouds suddenly grew black,   23
and the sun was gone. (S.I. 1.26)   27

    1 | 2 | 3 | 4 | 5 | 6 | 7 | 8 | 9 | 10 | 11 | 12 |

Record your progress   One minute

R.12   A thick haze covered the headland, and the wind, now at   11
gale force, was sharp and biting. Our pace was now slow and   23
in 2 hours we had covered only 3 miles - should we go on and   35
take a chance or turn back? (S.I. 1.13)   40

    1 | 2 | 3 | 4 | 5 | 6 | 7 | 8 | 9 | 10 | 11 | 12 |

Filling in form letters

The following steps should be taken when you fill in a form letter:

(a) Insert the form letter into the machine so that the first line of the body of the letter is just above the alignment scale.

(b) By means of the paper release, adjust the paper so that the base of the entire line is in alignment with the top of the alignment scale (this position may vary with certain makes of machines) and so that an 'i' or 'l' aligns up exactly with one of the white guides on the alignment scale.

(c) Set margin stops and paper guide. The margin stops should be set to correspond to the margins already used in the duplicated letter.

(d) Turn the cylinder back two single-line spaces (four notches for machines with half-spacing) and, if not already typed, insert salutation at the left-hand margin.

(e) Turn the cylinder back a sufficient number of spaces for the reference, name and address of the addressee and the spaces between, to reach the line for the reference.

(f) Type the reference.

(g) Turn up three single spaces and type the date.

(h) Turn up three single-line spaces and type the name and address of addressee.

(i) Insert any details required in the body of the letter. Remember to leave one clear space after the last character, before starting to type the 'fill in'.

(j) Check carefully.

---

2. Following the instructions given above, and using the original of the form letter prepared in Exercise 1 on page 114, insert the following details:

Your Ref. MAP/RES Our Ref. LEA/your initials Today's date

Addressee J. Ellis (Hardware) Ltd., 45—46 Warwick Road, Coventry. CV2 8UF

Invoice No. 5490 Dated (suitable date) for £260.50

---

3. On the carbon copy of the form letter prepared in Exercise 1 on page 114 insert the following details:

Your Ref. SW/SP Our Ref. LEA/your initials Today's date

Addressee Messrs. Barrett & Obrien, 17 Langley Road, Birmingham. B29 6PB

Invoice No. 3572 Dated (suitable date) for £945.74

Record your progress   3½ minutes

R.24   The number of guide cards used and their arrangement   10
depend on the filing system. The purpose of the guide cards   22
is, however, the same in all systems - to guide the eye when   34
finding and filing papers, and to support the folders. Guide   46
cards can be bought in all standard sizes, as well as for   58
special systems, such as fingerprint, hospital and insurance   70
files. Most guide cards have a tab along the top edge, and   81
this space contains a plain and clear reference to the folder   94
behind. It is important that this reference should be easy   105
to read, and it should give clear guidance to the order of   117
the folders. (S.I. 1.32)   120

1 | 2 | 3 | 4 | 5 | 6 | 7 | 8 | 9 | 10 | 11 | 12 |

Technique development

Typing fractions

Margins:
Elite 22—82
Pica 12—72

Practise [½] **and** [%] **key—; finger**

Practise ; to ½ back to ;

1. Type each of the following lines three times.

; ; ; ½½½ ; ; ; ½½½ ;½; ;½; 1½; 2½; 3½; 4½; 5½; 6½; 7½; 9½; 10½;

The prices are 2½p; 3½p; 4½p; 5½p; 6½p; 7½p; 8½p; 9½p; 10½p;

Depress left shift key for %

; ; ; %%% ; ; ; %%% ;%;% ;%;% 1%; 2%; 3%; 4%; 5%; 6%; 7%; 8%; 9%

Note: In addition to the ½ most typewriters have keys with other fractions. Examine your machine to find what fractions it has. These are all typed with the ½ finger. Some will require the use of the shift key. Practise the reaching movement from the home key to the fraction key you want to type. Remember: Always return your finger quickly to the home key.

; p¾; ; p¾; ; p¼; ; p¼; 1¾ 1¼ 2¾ 2¼ 3¾ 3¼ 4¾ 4¼ 5¾ 5¼ 6¾ 6¼ 17¾;

6¾ 6¼ 7¾ 7¼ 8¾ 8¼ 9¾ 9¼ 10¾ 10¼. Discount:- 33¾% plus 22½%;

Typing measurements

In typing measurements, note the following:

(a) The letter 'x' (*lower* case) is used for the word 'by'
Example: 210 mm × 297 mm (space before and after 'x').

(b) ONE space is left after the numbers and before the unit of measurement
Example: 210 (space) mm 2 (space) ft 6 (space) in.

(c) Groups of figures should not be separated at line-ends.

(d) Full stops are never used in abbreviations of metric measurements, but they may or may not be used in ft (feet) in (inches), etc. However, to be consistent, in this textbook we do not use a full stop after any abbreviated unit of measurement.

Note: Abbreviations do not take an 's' in the plural. e.g., 6 in 2 yd 6 lb 2 mm 4 kg

Practise typing measurements

2. Type each of the following lines three times on A5 landscape paper (210 × 148 mm), paying particular attention to spacing in measurements.

One room measures 180 cm × 120 cm; the other, 210 cm × 150 cm.
The carpets were all 6 ft 6 in × 5 ft 7 in or 6½ ft × 5½ ft.
Send me 5 lb of potatoes, 2 lb of sprouts, 3 lb of parsnips.

Use of words and figures

(a) Use words instead of figures for the number ONE on its own and numbers at the beginning of a sentence.
(b) Use figures in all other cases.

Note: These are the basic rules but your employer may sometimes instruct you differently. Publishers, for instance, often have their own rules.

Technique development

Form letters

Many firms use duplicated letters, printed forms, or postcards to send to customers. Details for each customer have to be filled in. Such letters or forms are known as 'Form Letters'. If details have to be filled in on ruled lines, or over dotted lines, it is essential that you type slightly above these lines.

Preparation of a form letter

1. Prepare the skeleton letter below, taking one carbon copy. To do this take the following steps:
   (a) Use A5 portrait paper.
   (b) Centre and type the name and address of the sender, starting on the fourth single space from top edge of paper.
   (c) Set margins at scale-points Elite 12–62, Pica 5–55.
   (d) After last line of sender's address turn up three single-line spaces and type *Your Ref.* at left margin.
   (e) Turn up one single-line space and type *Our Ref.* at left margin.
   (f) To allow for date, name and address of addressee and for two clear spaces after last line of address, turn up twelve single-line spaces.
   (g) Type *Dear Sirs* at left margin.
   (h) Turn up two single-line spaces and type remainder of letter, leaving clear spaces as indicated to accommodate the details given in Exercise 2 on page 115.

NEWTOWN WHOLESALE STORES LTD.
New Street, Sheffield. S5 8UP

(Turn up 3 spaces)

Your Ref.
Our Ref.

(Turn up 12 spaces)

Dear Sirs,

Please send us a copy of your invoice No. (leave blank)
dated (leave 16 spaces) for (leave 9 spaces) the receipt
of which we cannot trace. Your prompt attention
will be appreciated.

Yours faithfully,
NEWTOWN WHOLESALE STORES LTD.

Secretary

Technique development

Typing decimals

Margins: Elite 22—82
Pica 12—72

(a) Always use full stop for decimal point. This is usually typed in the normal position of a full stop.
(b) Leave NO space before or after decimal point.
(c) No punctuation required at end of figures except at the end of a sentence.
(d) Always insert the number of decimal places required by using zero.
Examples:
2 decimal places : type 86.40 NOT 86.4
3 decimal places: type 95.010 NOT 95.01

Practise typing decimals

1. Type each of the following sentences three times.

Add up 12.54, 13.02, 24.60, 6.75 and 0.20 and you get 57.11.

The sheet measures 1.200 × 5.810 × 2.540 m; the gross weight is approximately 50.802 kg and the nett weight is 38.102 kg.

Typing sums of money in context

(a) If the sum comprises only pounds, type as follows: £5, £10 or £5.00, £10.00
(b) If only pence, type: 10p 97p
Note: No space between figures and letter p, and no full stop after p (unless, of course, it ends a sentence).
(c) With mixed amounts, i.e., sums comprising pounds and pence, the decimal point and the £ symbol should always be used, but NOT the abbreviation p. Example: £7.05
(d) If the sum contains a decimal point but no whole pounds, a nought should be typed after the £ symbol and before the point. Example: £0.97
(e) The halfpenny is expressed by a fraction. Example: $3\frac{1}{2}$p or £0.03$\frac{1}{2}$

Practise typing sums of money in connected matter

2. Type the following in double-line spacing.

We thank you for your cheque for £20.10, and we enclose

our Credit Note for £0.50, which, together with our previous

Credit Note for £1.90, makes up the total amount of our last

invoice, viz. £22.50. Our present discount for cash monthly

is $2\frac{1}{2}$%.

Note use of words
and figures

As requested we are sending 10 copies of our latest

Bulletin No. 3. Two of these copies are to be retained by

you and the other 8 may be distributed among your clients.

Further exercises on words and figures are given on page 39 of **Practical Typing Exercises, Book One**

Skill building

In exercises A, B and C, type each line or sentence three times. If time permits, complete your practice by typing each group of lines as it appears. Keep your eyes on the copy and return the carriage sharply.

Margins:
Elite 22—82
Pica 12—72

A. Review alphabet keys

1. In view of the money embezzled by a junior employee, we must request you kindly to economise and avoid extravagance.

B. Improve control of shift key

2. Vale Kay Union Ruth Gwen Edna Lily Adam Nora Zena John Terry

3. York Coxon Olive Frank Henry Devon Innes Queen Wilson Barrie

4. Ask Miss Edna Terry to see Mr. P. St. John Coxon on Tuesday.

5. Adam, Olive, Frank, Lily and Ruth left Devon for York today.

C. Increase speed on common word drill

6. office where files have your were know are you did the as we

7. looked found there idea they left that not say had but no in

8. We know that the files were left in your office, but, as you say they are not there now, we have no idea where they are.

Accuracy practice	30 w.p.m. 3½ minutes	Not more than three errors

A.51   Throughout the ages leather has been used in countless   **11**
ways, and new methods of treating it have been found to make   **23**
it suitable for other uses. Primitive men used the skins   **34**
and hides of animals to provide themselves with warmth and   **46**
as protection against rocks and sharp thorns when they went   **58**
out to hunt for food. They also used them to keep themselves   **70**
warm at night.

    Today, although substitutes have been discovered, leather   **84**
is still much in demand, and for boots and shoes, for example,   **96**
it is also most durable and most reliable. (S.I. 1.35)   **105**

1 | 2 | 3 | 4 | 5 | 6 | 7 | 8 | 9 | 10 | 11 | 12 |

Speed Building	35 w.p.m. Two minutes	Not more than four errors

S.5   On checking your invoice, which has just reached us, we   **11**
find you have charged us the full list-price for items 4, 5,   **23**
and 6. No doubt this is due to a mistake on the part of one   **35**
of the clerks in your office, because, in the past, you have   **47**
charged us the wholesale rates. Please check this with your   **59**
books, and then send us a new invoice or a credit note.   **70**
    (S.I. 1.13)

S.6   When you walk through the woods you must look for a   **11**
very small plant that has green, glossy, oval-shaped leaves.   **23**
This plant does not grow very high. It has berries that are   **35**
a bright red colour and that stay there all the winter. The   **47**
name of this plant is the teaberry. Both berries and leaves   **59**
are quite pleasing to the taste, so we have been told.   **70**
    (S.I. 1.17)

1 | 2 | 3 | 4 | 5 | 6 | 7 | 8 | 9 | 10 | 11 | 12 |

Record your progress —page 115

UNIT 77

113

Consolidation

Production typing

When we look at a typewritten document our first impression is that it is well displayed or that it is badly displayed. We do not know, and we are not interested in, the speed at which it was typed. When reading the document we will notice errors in typing if there are any. Therefore, good display and accuracy are of the first importance. In addition, your employer, unlike the reader, is interested in the time you take to produce the document.

Putting the paper into your machine, deciding line-spacing and margins, setting tab stops for indentation, quick and accurate division of words at line-ends, all are essential typing techniques that require constant practice to ensure speed and accuracy. Your Production Target is the time you should take to complete each job of production typing. At first, you will reach this target only after concentrated practice. Watch and measure your progress by keeping each completed job in a Production Typing Folder. Type the date and the Production Target at the top of each job.

Job 1   Production Target—five minutes

Type the following exercise line for line on A5 portrait paper (148 × 210 mm). (a) Leave 25 mm (one inch) clear at top of page, i.e., turn up seven single-line spaces before you start to type. (b) Set margins at Elite 12–62, Pica 5–55. (c) Set tab stop for the indentation of the first line of each paragraph. (d) Use double-line spacing.

I recently saw some of the letters from rela-
tives. One lady wrote about her mother: "In one-
and-a-half years she had never had a cross word to
say about the treatment or staff. The sisters and
nurses on the ward were always kind."

Check your work

From my research into this matter, it is abun-
dantly clear that the patient - who for a year went
home at week-ends - had ample opportunity to com-
plain at home had she wished. She did not wish to
do so because she was most grateful for the kind-
ness she received while in hospital.

Job 2   Production Target—five minutes

Set out the following itinerary on a sheet of A5 landscape paper (210 × 148 mm). (a) Follow the display and layout exactly. (b) Centre the whole exercise vertically on the paper. (c) Use margins of Elite 22–82, Pica 12–72. (d) Centre main heading and sub-heading on typing line. (e) Leave three clear spaces between longest line of side headings and body. (f) Remember to set a tab stop for start of side headings, and set your left margin for start of body.

ITINERARY

Aberdeen/London - 2nd July, 1978

Aberdeen Airport   Check-in at 1800 hours
                      Take-off 1900 hours

London Airport   Arrive at 2030 hours
                      Single room booked at the Chester Hotel,
                      Highgate, for one night only

Important points to remember about inter-office memoranda:

(a) There are many different layouts for headings.
(b) There is no salutation.
(c) To ensure proper alignment when typing over dotted lines, use the variable line-spacer.
(d) When typing over dotted lines, the typing must be just slightly above the dots so that no part of a character touches the dotted line.
(e) Leave two clear spaces before typing after words in printed heading. This must be consistent for all headings.
(f) The subject heading may start two clear spaces after the word SUBJECT in order to be consistent with the spacing of the other details, or it may be centred.
(g) Margins: Elite 12–90, Pica 10–75. These margins may, however, vary according to the size of the form.
(h) Start to type body of memo two single-line spaces below the word SUBJECT.
(i) Paragraphs may be indented or in block form.
(j) Body of memo is typed in single spacing with double spacing between paragraphs.
(k) No complimentary closing and usually no signature.
(l) If an enclosure is mentioned in a memo, this is indicated in the usual way (as in a business letter) by typing *Enc.* (or *Encs.* if more than one enclosure) at the left margin.

Further practice in typing memoranda

3. Using the two carbon memos prepared in Exercise 1 on page 111, insert the following details:

(a) To Personnel Officer   From General Manager   Today's date
Subject   STAFF MEETING

A meeting will be held in the Conference Room on Monday afternoon at 5 o'clock. Will you please advise all members of the clerical staff that they are expected to attend the meeting.

(b) To Sales Manager   From Managing Director   Today's date
Subject   COMPLAINTS

It has come to my notice that orders received from customers are not being acknowledged promptly. Please look into this and report to me immediately as to the accuracy of the complaint.

Further exercises in typing memoranda are given on pages 48 and 49 of
Practical Typing Exercises, Book One

Record your progress   Three minutes

R.23   We thank you for your request for a copy of our latest   11
list, but have to state that we do not issue a general cata-   23
logue, in view of the improvements which we make in our   34
products from time to time, and we feel that any benefits   45
should be passed on at once to our customers. We are send-   57
ing you a few brochures which give full descriptions of some   69
of our standard lines, and also details of our prices and   80
terms of delivery. Our agent, Mr. F. A. Clarke, hopes to be   92
in Inverness from 26th to 31st May, and would be pleased to   104
call on you to help in any way he can. (S.I. 1.28)   112

    1 | 2 | 3 | 4 | 5 | 6 | 7 | 8 | 9 | 10 | 11 | 12 |

Display the following menu on a sheet of A5 portrait paper (148 × 210 mm).
(a) Centre each line horizontally and the whole exercise vertically.
(b) Please type the separate courses in single spacing, and leave three clear spaces between each course, i.e., turn up four single-line spaces.
(c) Before starting to type, prepare a layout showing where you will use spaced capitals, closed capitals, underscore, and the space to be left between horizontal lines.

Check your typing very carefully before removing paper from machine

Palace Hotel
Blackpool
M E N U
Dinner

Tomato Soup
Chilled Melon

Roast Beef and Yorkshire Pudding
Creamed Potatoes
Carrots/Beans/Cabbage
Horseradish Sauce

Chocolate Gateau
Apple Pie and Fresh Cream
Ice Cream

Coffee

Type the following exercise on A5 landscape paper (210 × 148 mm).
(a) Leave 25 mm (one inch) clear at top of page. (b) Use margins of Elite 22–82, Pica 12–72. (c) Centre main heading on typing line. (d) Set tab stop for indentation of the first line of each paragraph. (e) Use single spacing with double between paragraphs. (f) Use paragraph headings as in copy. Remember to underscore a paragraph heading. (g) See that you leave *two clear spaces* after full stop which follows paragraph heading.

SPECIAL CONDITIONS OF PURCHASE

Quotations. These shd be submitted in triplicate and on the contractors' printed headings. Prices shd be in the currency of the country of origin.

Delivery. The delivery period of the equipment forming the subject of the order shd be indicated, + this shd be firm f 30 days.

Payment. Our conditions of payment are: 80% against shipping docs. + 20% on the starting up of the installation + after the approval of our engineers has bn obtained.

Technique development

Inter-office memoranda

A message from one person to another in the same firm, or from the Head Office to a branch office, or to an agent, is often in the form of a memorandum—usually referred to as a 'memo'. Inter-office memoranda may be typed on any of the usual sizes of paper. The layout may vary from organisation to organisation.

Preparation of memo form

1. If you do not have memo forms with printed headings, prepare your own. Take three sheets of A5 landscape paper and interleave with two sheets of carbon paper, then proceed as follows:
   (a) Centre and type the word MEMORANDUM on the fourth single-line space from the top.
   (b) Turn up two single spaces.
   (c) Set margins at Elite 12–90, Pica 10–75.
   (d) At left margin type the word To followed by one space and unspaced dots to scale-point 55 (elite), 45 (pica). On same line at scale-point 60 (elite), 50 (pica), type the word Date followed by one clear space and unspaced dots to scale-point 90 (elite), 75 (pica) (right-hand margin).
   (e) Turn up two single spaces and type the word From at margin followed by one clear space and unspaced dots to scale-point 55 (elite), 45 (pica).
   (f) Turn up one space and type underscore from scale-point 3 (elite), 2 (pica), to scale-point 96 (elite), 80 (pica).
   (g) Turn up two spaces and type the word Subject at margin followed by one clear space and unspaced dots to right-hand margin.

Variable line-spacer

The variable line-spacer is found on the left cylinder knob. By pressing this in or pulling it out, the platen roller can be moved to any position desired. Its purpose is to ensure that you have proper alignment of the details to be typed on dotted lines, ruled lines, or when completing a form letter.

Practise typing memorandum

2. Type the following memo on a printed memo form or on the original prepared in Exercise 1 above. Type slightly above the dotted lines by using the variable line-spacer.

MEMORANDUM

To .Head.of.Training.School...............   Date .2nd.February,.1978......

From .General.Manager.....................

_____

(Turn up 2 single-line spaces)

Subject .STYLE.OF.LETTERS...

It has now been decided that all departments should use the block style of letters. Please, therefore, give instructions to all office trainees to adopt this style in future. For their guidance, the attached specimen should be affixed to the notice board.

Enc.

Note: If pica type is being used, line-endings will differ from above.

UNIT 76

Type the following exercise on A5 landscape paper (210 × 148 mm).
(a) Leave 25 mm (one inch) clear at top of page. (b) Use margins of Elite 20–85, Pica 10–75. (c) Centre main heading on typing line. (d) Start the first line of each paragraph at the margin and use hanging paragraphs.

INSTRUCTIONS

How well do you follow instructions? Employers & examiners tell us th, f some unknown reason, typists tend to ignore instructions.

We must impress upon you th on every occasion it is essential th y carry out all instructions exactly as stated. At business it may be th y find the instructions are not quite clear. In such a case, ask the person concerned to be kind enough to clarify his directions.

It is imperative th y read all instructions before starting to type. NEVER, in any circumstances, type fr a manuscript exercise w'out first reading it through.

Note to typist - Please type the above exercise in single spacing with double between paras.

Type the following exercise on A4 paper (210 × 297 mm).
(a) Leave 25 mm (one inch) clear at top of page. (b) Set margins at Elite 20–85, Pica 10–75. (c) Centre main headings on typing line. (d) Use block paragraphs. (e) Set out shoulder headings as in copy. (f) Type abbreviations in full where necessary.

USE OF TELEPHONE

You must be certain th you know the correct no. you wish to dial. Where you need to dial a code before the no. you want, check this in the dialling instructions & make a note of the code and no. before you dial.

DIAL

When you hear the dialling tone place yr finger in the correct no., turn the dial firmly round to the stop & let it return by itself. Do this for each figure th you need to dial.

ANSWERING CALLS

Answer yr telephone w'out delay, giving yr name, the name of yr firm or yr own no. If when you pick up the receiver you hear a series of rapid pips, this means th the call is coming fr a coinbox. You must then wait for the caller to insert the money, &, when the pips stop, the caller will be able to hear you.

Skill building

Type each exercise (A, B and C) three times. Keep your eyes on the copy and return the carriage sharply.

Margins:
Elite 22—82
Pica 12—72

A. Review alphabet keys

1. These 2 travellers were sorely vexed and puzzled by the rapturous welcome they had just been given by the quiet, but kind, official.

B. Build accuracy on one-hand words

2. dresses nylon extra jolly great knoll agree pylon gave on my

3. opinion trade union aware only safe upon area joy car him at

4. In our opinion, you were aware of the trade union wage rate.

5. I agree the extra trade in nylon dresses gave him great joy.

C. Improve control of double-letter words

6. programmes possible running supply arrive proof agree added.

7. difficult football baggage accept excess rubber attend carry

8. Is it possible to supply a proof of the football programmes?

9. We agree that it was difficult to accept the excess baggage.

Accuracy practice	30 w.p.m. Three minutes	Not more than three errors

A.50   When you have regular payments to make each month or   10
each quarter, as, for instance, for rent, rates, car insur-   22
ance, there is no need for you to make out a cheque each   33
time. It will be quite simple for you to give a standing   44
order to your bank to pay such amounts on your behalf until   56
further notice, and these sums will be placed to the debit   68
of your account each month or quarter, as the case may be.   80
This method will save you a great deal of trouble. (S.I. 1.22)   90

    1 | 2 | 3 | 4 | 5 | 6 | 7 | 8 | 9 | 10 | 11 | 12 |

Speed building	35 w.p.m. 1½ minutes	Not more than three errors

S.3   The repairs to your car have been put in hand, but they   11
will take 2 or 3 weeks. In spite of this, we shall be able   23
to have the car ready for you by the date required. We have   35
no doubt that you will be quite pleased with the quality and   47
standard of the work done. (S.I. 1.13)   52

S.4   Your name has now been put on our mailing list, and we   11
shall send you a copy of all our leaflets. We shall also be   23
pleased to let you have any details you like regarding the   35
work we do. Please get in touch with us if you think we can   47
be of help to you in any way. (S.I. 1.17)   52

    1 | 2 | 3 | 4 | 5 | 6 | 7 | 8 | 9 | 10 | 11 | 12 |

Record your progress —page 112

Getting letters ready for the post

In many offices, letters have to be typed ready for signature by a certain time in the morning and/or afternoon. This is to allow ample time for gathering together any enclosures, and for stamping or franking to catch the evening mail.

Procedures for passing letters for signature vary from firm to firm: some employers require the originals and carbon copies; others want to see only originals. Whatever method is adopted, you must see that any additions or deletions in the originals are also made on the carbon copies before the originals are mailed.

If possible, always attach enclosures to the letter before it is sent for signature. If this is not done (e.g., bulky items such as samples) see that the enclosure is inserted with the letter when it has been signed.

When the signed letters are returned—

1. Check to see that carbon copies have, where necessary, been amended.

2. Check inside address on the letter with that on envelope.

3. Check to see that all enclosures are inserted.

4. Fill the envelope, but do not seal down until you have completed the filling, so that, if you have made a mistake, you will not have to unseal any envelopes.

5. Seal all envelopes ready for posting.

6. Arrange carbon copies in sorting file ready for filing.

Review Quiz No. 2

1. In blocked paragraphs all lines start at the . . . . . .

2. Indented paragraphs are typed in . . . or . . . spacing and the first line is indented . . . spaces from . . . margin.

3. When double-line spacing is used in block paragraphs, turn up . . . single line spaces between the paragraphs.

4. In hanging paragraphs the second and subsequent lines start . . . spaces to the . . . of the first line.

5. The main heading of a passage may be typed in the . . . of the typing line or . . . at left margin.

6. If spaced capitals are used, leave . . . space between each letter and . . . spaces between each word.

7. If closed capitals are used, . . . space is left between letters but . . . space between words.

8. Sub-headings may be . . . at left margin or . . . in typing line and separated from main heading by . . . blank line.

9. After the sub-heading turn up . . . single line spaces.

10. If a heading is typed in lower case letters, it must be . . .

11. Paragraph headings may be in . . . or . . . style.

12. A shoulder heading is typed in . . . capitals at . . . margin and is usually preceded and followed by . . . blank line.

13. Side headings are typed . . . the left margin and usually in . . . capitals with or without . . .

14. When underscoring do . . . underscore final punctuation mark.

15. In typing measurements . . . space is left . . . the number and . . . the unit of measurement.

16. The word 'by' is expressed by the letter . . . in . . . case.

17. Full stops are . . . used in abbreviations of metric measurements.

18. The abbreviated forms of yards, inches, etc., do . . . take an 's' in the plural.

Turn to page 151 and check your answers. Score one point for each correct entry.
Total score: 36.

Note: There is no definite rule about the number of spaces to be left between columns. This depends on the total width of the table. It is recommended that three or five spaces should be left, so that the columns may be separated sufficiently from each other and yet be close enough to make them easily read. If five spaces are left between columns in a boxed table with closed sides, the horizontal lines should extend three spaces (instead of two) beyond the left margin and three spaces beyond the last character in the last column.

4. Type the following on A5 landscape paper (210 × 148 mm) in double spacing, leaving 5 spaces between columns. Centre the table horizontally and vertically. Use centred or blocked style.

MARCH TEMPERATURE

l.c. TOWN	Conditions	Centigrade	Fahrenheit
Berlin	Fair	12	54
Dublin	Fair	9	48
Edinburgh	Fair	9	48
London	Rain	7	45
New York	Rain	9	48
Paris	Rain	9	48
Rome	Sunny	17	63

Further exercises on boxed tables are given on pages 34—37 of **Practical Typing Exercises, Book One**

Record your progress   2½ minutes

R.22   Added to the return which the owner of a business gets   11
for the use of his office, his work, and the cash he has put   23
into it, he hopes to gain a profit. Profit is the amount   34
that is left when all costs, even those which have been   45
supplied by the owner, have been paid for. Pure profits are   57
the reward he hopes to get for all the risks he has to take   69
by gambling on the success, or failure, of his venture.   80

(S.I. 1.23)

1 | 2 | 3 | 4 | 5 | 6 | 7 | 8 | 9 | 10 | 11 | 12 |

Type each exercise (A, B, and C) three times. Keep your eyes on the copy and return the carriage sharply.

A. Review alphabet keys

Margins:
Elite 22—82
Pica 12—72

1.   A falling off in zinc supplies last July will have been noted, and prices may be expected to rise generally.

B. Improve control of figure keys

2. ewe 323 woe 293 our 974 rye 463 you 697 tour 5974 writ 2485.

3. Type 1 and 2 and 3 and 4 and 15 and 16 and 17 and 80 and 90.

4. Drill: 10, 29, 38, 47, 56, 234, 567, 890, 010, 343, 678, 86.

5. Accounts: 00-11-2345, 00-12-6789, 00-13-5858, 00-14-2679-80.

C. Build accuracy on punctuation review

6. "Is John - John Mann, not John Green - here, please?" "No."

7. We discussed many things: the staff; an up-to-date building; annual holidays. "What happened then?" "We did not agree."

8. I think (in fact I'm sure) that Mr. Laing will arrive today.

Accuracy/speed practice   27 w.p.m.   1½ minutes   Not more than one error

A/S.27   Did you know that you could be taken to court and fined   11
for being too close to the car in front? It is not easy for   23
us to judge distance, but the Highway Code offers some help,   35
and we should all read it. **(S.I. 1.15)**   40

A/S.28   At present there is no aid with which to judge the dis-   11
tance from the roadside or from a car in front. However, we   23
know that a device is being made that will help us gauge how   35
far we are from other cars. **(S.I. 1.20)**   40

A/S.29   Until this device is fitted to all cars, you must learn   11
to drive with care and leave plenty of space between you and   23
a vehicle in front so that you can stop and not cause damage   35
to any other road users. **(S.I. 1.27)**   40

    1 | 2 | 3 | 4 | 5 | 6 | 7 | 8 | 9 | 10 | 11 | 12 |

Record your progress   1½ minutes

R.13   Have you ever been to a large airport just to watch the   11
endless movement of people and planes? You can see hundreds   23
of folks get on or off a huge new jet, and it makes you won-   35
der how this plane ever gets into the air or lands so grace-   47
fully. Visit an airport. **(S.I. 1.25)**   52

    1 | 2 | 3 | 4 | 5 | 6 | 7 | 8 | 9 | 10 | 11 | 12 |

UNIT 48

Boxed table with closed sides

If the left and right sides of a table are required to be closed by vertical lines, these should be ruled from the end of the horizontal lines as in the table in Exercise 2 below.

Ruling in ink

Both horizontal lines and vertical lines may be ruled by typewriter or in ink, or the horizontal lines may be ruled by typewriter and the vertical lines in ink. If ink ruling only is used, proceed as follows:

(a) Mark the beginning and end of each horizontal line either in pencil or by striking the underscore lightly. This will make a light mark which can easily be covered by the ink ruling.

(b) Mark the scale-points at which the vertical lines are to be ruled (i.e., half-way between the longest item of one column and the start of the next) along the top and bottom horizontal lines by striking the underscore lightly. The vertical lines should be ruled from the *middle* of the underscore (except those at the *beginning* and *end* of each horizontal line, which should be ruled from the outer edge of the underscore).

(c) Rule the vertical before the horizontal lines, so that the guide marks are not covered up.

(d) Pencil ruling is not acceptable.

Practise typing boxed table with closed sides

2. Type the following table on A5 portrait paper (148 × 210 mm) in double spacing, leaving three spaces between columns. Use centred or block style. Centre the table horizontally and vertically, and rule.

BUSINESS TERMS

Insurance	Legal	Stock Exchange
Endowment	Affidavit	Jobber
Insurer	Attestation	Stockbroker
Insured	Endorsement	Option
Policy	Engrossment	Gilt-edged
Premium	Indenture	Bulls
Proposal Form	Testator	Bears

3. Type the following boxed table in double spacing with closed sides on A5 landscape paper (210 × 148 mm). Leave three spaces between columns. Rule horizontal lines by underscore and vertical lines in ink.

WORLD CURRENCIES

Exchange Rates - subject to fluctuation

Country	Monetary unit	Units per £ sterling	Units per US $
Belgium	Franc	55.50	43.90
Denmark	Krone	14.89	6.85
Germany	Deutschmark	6.17	2.64
Portugal	Escudo	58.75	24.00
Spain	Peseta	124.25	58.50
United States	Dollar	2.18	—

Technique Development

Layout of business letters

Letters are an ambassador and an advertisement for the firm sending them. You must, therefore, ensure that *your* letters are well displayed and faultlessly typed. Although each firm may have its own method of display, the following illustrate the principal business letter styles.

Fully blocked
Note: This is often known as 'blocked'. Begin *every* line at the left margin.

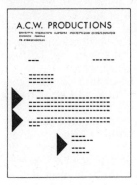

Semi-blocked
Date and complimentary closing as shown, with first line of each paragraph indented.

Parts of a business letter

General layout

1. *Reference*
   (a) Dictator's and typist's initials identify the department or person dictating the letter.
   (b) Type at left margin.
   (c) Note differing styles shown in specimen letters.
   (d) Sometimes typed in lower left corner.

2. *Date*
   (a) Correct order is day, month, year.
   (b) Never abbreviate the date.

3. *Addressee*
   (a) Turn up three single-line spaces after reference and date, and type inside name and address.
   (b) Begin at left margin.
   (c) Inside address is blocked.

4. *Salutation*
   (a) Turn up three single-line spaces after inside address and type salutation.
   (b) Begin typing at left margin.
   (c) First letter of each word in capitals.

5. *Body of letter*
   (a) Type in single-line spacing, with double-line spacing between paragraphs.
   (b) If short letter, semi-blocked, type in double-line spacing, with double-line spacing between paragraphs.
   (c) Turn up two single-line spaces after salutation and begin typing body of letter.

6. *Complimentary closing*
   Turn up two single-line spaces after last line of body of letter and type complimentary closing.

7. *Signature*
   (a) Turn up one single-line space after complimentary closing.
   (b) Begin typing name of firm at same point as beginning of complimentary closing.

8. *Designation*
   (a) If person signing has official position, turn up a minimum of five single-line spaces to leave room for signature.
   (b) Begin typing the official position at the same scale-point as the complimentary closing.

Open punctuation

Many organisations are now using open punctuation in business letters. This means that no punctuation is inserted in the reference, date, name and address of addressee, salutation, complimentary close and any wording below.
In the body of the letter the normal punctuation is used in sentences except in the following cases:

1. Where an abbreviation ends in a full stop, the full stop is omitted and replaced by a space. Example: Mr (space) J (space) Smith, our Managing Director, will call on Tuesday next to discuss the question of deliveries, terms of payment, etc, to which you referred in your letter.

2. Where an abbreviation consists of two or more letters with a full stop after each letter, the full stops are omitted and no space is left between the letters, but one space (or comma) after the group of letters. Example: There are a number of local broadcasting stations eg, Radio Derby, BRMB, etc.

3. The normal practice is to omit *th*, etc., in dates.

Technique development

Boxed table—open sides

A boxed table has vertical lines between the columns in addition to horizontal lines. The left and right sides may or may not be closed in by vertical lines. The vertical lines between the columns must be ruled exactly in the middle of each blank space. It is therefore advisable to leave an odd number of spaces between the columns—one for the vertical ruling, and an equal number on either side of the ruling. To rule the vertical lines, take the following steps:

(a) First set left margin for start of first column, tab stops for the remaining columns, and right-hand margin as explained on page 99 (c).

(b) After typing main heading, return carriage to left margin and type first horizontal line as explained on page 99 (e).

(c) Move to first tab stop and backspace two; at this point make a pencil mark for the first vertical line.

(d) Move to next tab stop and backspace two; at this point make a pencil mark for the second vertical line.

(e) Continue in the same way for any additional column.

(f) When you have typed the horizontal line at the bottom of the table, mark in pencil the bottom of each of the vertical lines.

To rule vertical lines by means of the underscore, take the paper out of the machine and re-insert it sideways, taking care to see that the paper is straight. Do not allow the vertical lines to extend above or below the horizontal lines. They must meet precisely. To enable you to adjust the platen roller easily, in order to find the points marked for the vertical lines, release the interliner lever (see page 105).

Practise typing 'boxed' table with open sides

1. Type the following boxed table in double spacing on A5 landscape paper (210 × 148 mm), leaving three spaces between columns. Use underscore for horizontal and vertical lines. Use blocked or centred style.

NETT TURNOVER FOR 6 MONTHS ENDED 30TH JUNE

Month	Clothing	Footwear	Total
	£	£	£
January	940.50	646.00	2553.45
February	1532.75	1020.70	1642.65
March	827.30	815.35	2337.10
April	1215.50	1121.60	1718.55
May	964.25	754.30	1754.80
June	745.60	1009.20	1586.50
TOTAL	6225.90	5367.15	11593.05

Further exercises on Boxed Table with open sides are given on page 33 of **Practical Typing Exercises, Book One**

Letter heading

When typing letters, if you are not using paper with printed heading:
    On A5 paper turn up six single-line spaces
    On A4 paper turn up nine single-line spaces
to represent the heading. Then turn up another three single-line spaces before typing reference or date. If you are using headed paper turn up three single-line spaces after last line of heading.

Fully-blocked letters

As shown in the illustration on page 62, every line in a fully-blocked letter begins at the left margin.

Practise typing fully-blocked letter

1. After studying the layout of the following specimen letter, type it on A5 portrait paper (148 × 210 mm). Keep to the spacing and layout indicated. Set margins at Elite 12—62; Pica 5—55. Use open punctuation.

(Turn up 9 single-line spaces)

1. Reference   Our Ref HGS/HOS

(Turn up 3 single-line spaces)

2. Date   20 October 1977

(Turn up 3 single-line spaces)

3. Addressee   N J Johnson & Co Ltd
24 High Street
BRADFORD
West Yorkshire   BD4 9HU

Leave six spaces between town (or county) and postcode and one space between the two halves of the code

(Turn up 3 single-line spaces)

4. Salutation   Dear Sirs

(Turn up 2 single-line spaces)

5. Body of letter   Our representative, Mr J Smith, will be in your district next week, and will take the opportunity of calling on you on Wednesday next at 10 am.

(Turn up 2 single-line spaces)

If this date is not suitable, will you please let us know when it will be convenient for you to see Mr Smith.

(Turn up 2 single-line spaces)

6. Complimentary close   Yours faithfully   (Turn up 1 single-line space)
MIDLAND FURNITURE CO LTD

7. Signature   (Turn up 5 single-line spaces)

8. Name   H G SIMMONS   (Turn up 1 single-line space)
9. Designation   Sales Department

Tabulation with columns of figures

When columns in a table contain figures, care must be taken to see that units come under units, tens under tens, etc. Where numbers comprise five figures or less these may be blocked together (without the use of a comma to separate thousands from hundreds). Where, however, there are six or more figures, these are grouped in threes starting from the unit figure, a space being left between each group instead of a comma being used.

NOTE: If any number in any column of a table contains six or more figures, all groups must be in threes even though the column may contain items of less than six figures.

Practise typing figures in columns

Note: If blocked method is used in tabulation, the £ sign is blocked at the tab stop set for the longest item. See exercise 3 below.

3. After studying the above explanation, type the following table on A5 landscape paper (210 × 148 mm). Use double spacing and rule horizontal lines. Centre table horizontally and vertically. Block or centre headings. Leave three spaces between columns.

COMPARATIVE DEPARTMENTAL TURNOVER

Department	1974	1975	1976
	£	£	£
Clothing	114 320	196 400	212 345
Furniture	1 100 450	2 368 500	2 432 546
Kitchen Utensils	800 000	909 120	345 625
Hardware	523 412	619 345	800 050
TOTAL	2 538 182	4 093 365	3 790 566

4. Type the following table on A5 landscape paper (210 × 148 mm). Use double-line spacing and rule horizontal lines. Centre table horizontally and vertically, leaving 3 spaces between columns. Use block or centred headings.

WEEKLY REPAYMENTS OF LOAN IN £'S

Amount of loan	3 years	5 years	7 years
300	2.57	1.83	1.50
500	4.29	3.06	2.50
750	6.43	4.59	3.76
1000	8.28	5.90	4.90
1500	12.57	8.86	7.35
2000	16.77	11.81	9.80

2. Type the following letter on A5 portrait paper (148 × 210 mm), keeping to the spacing and layout. Set margins at Elite 12–62, Pica 5–55.

(Turn up 9 single-line spaces)

Our Ref HJB/RAT

4 November 1977

Midland Furniture Co Ltd
Broad Street
BURTON ON TRENT
Staffordshire   DE14 1RF

Dear Sirs

On 8 October last we ordered 60 chairs from your
representative, delivery of which was promised for
30 October, but up to the present date we have not
yet received them.

We would therefore ask you to look into the matter
and let us know when we may expect delivery of the
chairs in question.

Yours faithfully
N J JOHNSON & CO LTD

H J Bates
Purchase Manager

3. Type the following letter on A5 portrait paper (148 × 210 mm) in fully-blocked style. Set margins at Elite 12–62, Pica 5–55.

Our Ref HGS/HOS   5 November 1977
N J Johnson & Co Ltd   24 High Street Bradford
                        West Yorkshire BD4 9HU
Dear Sirs
In reply to yr ltr of 4 Nov, we are now arranging to deliver
on Monday next, 8 Nov the 60 chairs wh yr recently ordered
fr us, & must apologise f the delay in despatch.
We now look forward to receiving the order f the Tables
and desks abt wh yr consulted us.
Yours ffly   MIDLAND FURNITURE CO LTD
H G Simmons   Sales Department

Technique development

Typing sums of money in columns

Refer to the instructions given on page 56 with regard to the typing of decimals. Then note the following:

When typing columns of money items, two figures must appear in the pence after the decimal point, and the £ sign should be centred over the unit figure of the pounds. If the item comprises pounds only, centre the £ sign over the longest line in the column.

Example:

```
    £
110.05
 20.00
  0.10
 13.72
```

Practise typing sums of money in columns

1. Type the following in double spacing on A5 portrait paper (148 × 210 mm), leaving five spaces between columns. Do not rule.

£	£	£
146.57	1358.25	216.90
200.06	347.12	325.89
19.55	420.75	1100.00
254.56	567.89	1337.90

Interliner lever

The interliner lever is usually on the left side of the carriage. Locate this on your machine. (It is sometimes known as 'ratchet release'.) The interliner lever frees the cylinder from the ratchet control, so that the cylinder may be turned freely forward or backward as required. When the lever is returned to its normal position, your machine will automatically return to the original line of writing.

Double underscoring of totals

If you have to type double lines underneath the totals, use the interliner. When typing totals proceed as follows:

(a) Type the underscore for the first line above the total (Do not turn up before typing the first line.)
(b) Turn up twice and type the total.
(c) Turn up once, and then type the line below the total.
(d) Turn the cylinder up slightly by using the interliner lever and type the double line. Then return the interliner lever to its normal position.

Note: The underscore should not extend above or below the £ sign.

Practise typing double lines under totals

2. Display the following on A5 landscape paper (210 × 148 mm). Type horizontal lines with underscore, using interliner for double total lines. Leave three spaces between columns.

£	£	£	£
228.90	12.34	212.34	109.87
404.75	566.78	33.44	654.57
323.25	90.12	105.62	1010.85
1234.56	35.45	1212.05	354.25
789.00	1237.95	343.18	1213.65
654.32	220.16	331.26	434.12
£3634.78	£2162.80	£2237.89	£3777.31

For further exercises on double underscore of totals see page 37 of **Practical Typing Exercises, Book One**

Technique development

For the attention of . . .

Many companies adopt the rule that all correspondence should be addressed to the company and not to individual persons by name. The sender of a letter may wish it to reach or be dealt with by a particular person or department. This is indicated by typing the words 'For the attention of . . .' on a separate line on the letter two spaces below the inside address. Turn up *TWO* single-line spaces between this instruction and the salutation, *which should be 'Dear Sirs,'.*

Enclosures

The inclusion of papers or documents in a letter is indicated by typing the abbreviation 'Enc.' (with or without underscore) at the left-hand margin at least two single-line spaces below the designation. This helps to ensure that *all* documents are included in the envelope for posting.

Practise typing letter with 'Attention' line and Enclosure

1. Type the following letter on A4 paper (210 × 297 mm) in fully-blocked style, using margins Elite 27–77, Pica 18–68. Turn up 12 single-line spaces from top edge of paper.

Ref ABC/DEF

24 January 1977

Midland Furniture Co Ltd
Broad Street
BURTON ON TRENT
Staffordshire
DE14 1RF
           (Turn up 2 single-line spaces)
<u>For the attention of Mr J White</u>
           (Turn up 2 single-line spaces)
Dear Sirs

We enclose a cheque for £126.75 in settlement of the attached statement. You will notice that we have deducted the sum of £3.25, representing 2½% discount, as in your letter of 31 May 1976 you agreed to allow us this discount for prompt payment.

Will you please confirm that you will continue to allow us this cash discount.

Yours faithfully
N J JOHNSON & CO LTD

A B Cooke
Secretary
        (Turn up a minimum of 2 single-line spaces)
Enc

In exercises A, B and C, type each line or sentence three times. If time permits, complete your practice by typing each group of lines as it appears. Keep your eyes on the copy and return the carriage sharply.

Margins:
Elite 22—82
Pica 12—72

A.   Review alphabet keys

1.   The Principals soon realized that extra milk would have to be requisitioned each morning for the lively young pupils in the junior school.

B.   Build speed on word family drill

2. look took hook book nook cook best pest rest jest west nest.

3. call hall fall pall wall tall will pill bill hill fill mill.

4. He took a look at the book and said that he would call soon.

5. The birds will nest in a nook of the west wall of that mill.

C.   Build speed on fluency drill

6. right both they land wish held firm hand sign paid when form

7. busy lane fork pays dial make rich maps with half fuel road.

8. They wish both firms to sign the forms and pay for the land.

9. It is a busy lane to the right of a fork road by the chapel.

Accuracy/speed practice

Speed can be built up more easily on short, simple, exercises, and, as we have now reached 2½ minutes at 30 w.p.m., and will continue at 30 w.p.m. with increased length of timing, in this and subsequent Skill Building Units we are separating the accuracy and the speed. You may wish to practise the accuracy or the speed, or perhaps both. As a guide, we would suggest that, if you have more than one error for each minute typed, then you should continue with the Accuracy Practice. If you have less than one error for each minute typed, you may wish to build your speed by using this Speed Building material.

Accuracy practice   30 w.p.m.   2½ minutes   Not more than two errors

A.49   The Chairman of the Board has written to me to say that   11
Mr. T. Young has been badly hurt in an accident, and that he   23
will not be at work for at least 18 months. You are aware,   35
no doubt, of the fact that he has a large number of speaking   47
engagements in many different cities, and these will have to   59
be cancelled at once unless we are able to engage someone to   71
take over from him. (S.I. 1.24)   75

      1 | 2 | 3 | 4 | 5 | 6 | 7 | 8 | 9 | 10 | 11 | 12 |

Speed building   35 w.p.m.   One minute   Not more than two errors

S.1   In the spring we always go to a farm, where we are made   11
most welcome. We are allowed to do more or less as we like,   23
and we have a fine time. We often wish we could live there.   35
                                                    (S.I. 1.11)

S.2   Once a month most firms send to each of their customers   11
a statement which shows how much they owe to the firm at the   23
end of the month. It also shows the trade during the month.   35
                                                    (S.I. 1.14)

      1 | 2 | 3 | 4 | 5 | 6 | 7 | 8 | 9 | 10 | 11 | 12 |

Record your progress —page 109

In fully-blocked letters the date may be typed to end level with the right-hand margin as in Exercise 2 below, and typed on the same line as the reference. To find starting point for the date, backspace from right margin one space for each character and space in the date.

2. Type the following letter on A4 paper (210 × 297 mm) in fully-blocked style, using margins of Elite 27–77, Pica 18–68.

(Turn up 12 single-line spaces)

Ref AWC/FA   28 March 1977

William Newman & Co Ltd
Park Road
SOUTH CROYDON
Surrey   CR2 8JJ

For the attention of Mr James Wilson

Dear Sirs

We thank you for your verbal enquiry of 26 March, and, as requested, have pleasure in enclosing a leaflet which gives a description of the machines we have for sale. On our printed prices we are prepared to allow you a trade discount of 15%.

We look forward to hearing from you when you have had an opportunity to peruse the leaflet enclosed.

Yours faithfully
MIDLAND FURNITURE CO LTD

A W Clifford
Machinery Department

Enc

3. Type the following letter on A4 paper (210 × 297 mm) in fully-blocked style, using margins of Elite 27–77, Pica 18–68. Open punctuation. Mark 'For the attention of Mr J Hill'. Abbreviations to be typed in full.

Ref JAH/LMN   Insert today's date (at right margin)

R G Lewis & Co Ltd   North Street   Bradford   BD4 9HU

Dear Sirs   We are advised by our York Branch Manager th our Central Heating System has bn installed in yr offices, & we now hv pleasure in enclosing our   a/c for the amt due. [We feel sure y wl find this system to be most helpful both in relation to comfort + utility.

Yrs ffy B HADLEY (CENTRAL HEATING) LTD
Enc   J A HARRIS   SECRETARY

Typist:
[= New paragraph

Office Stationery

Many firms have the rule that stationery supplies must be requisitioned on definite dates or at certain times. Arrange your own supplies neatly in the drawers of your desk or in your cupboard. If at any time you notice that you need fresh supplies of a particular item, enter full details at once in your desk diary under the next requisition date. This will save time and ensure that the item is not forgotten. When making out your requisition form, it is helpful to affix a specimen of the stationery you require. The good secretary always has the necessary tools to do her work properly.

Review Quiz No. 4

1. The abbreviation & is known as the . . . and is used in names of . . . and in . . .

2. A new paragraph is indicated by . . . or . . .

3. The caret sign means that words omitted are to be . . . and *of* means that the letter or word is to be . . .

4. To centre columns horizontally first clear all . . . . . . and . . .

5. When inserting paper, see that the left edge is at . . . on carriage scale.

6. To determine starting point for each column, backspace . . . for every . . . . . . and . . . in the longest item of each column.

7. The longest line of a column may be in the . . . or in the column . . .

8. Set . . . . . . for start of first column and . . . . . . for start of each of the other columns.

9. When using block style for column display, type main heading at . . . . . .

10. Turn up . . . single-line spaces after main heading.

11. To centre columns vertically count the number of lines to be typed and the . . . between the lines.

12. Divide the difference found in (11) above by . . . ignoring . . . Begin to type table on . . . line.

13. Usually it is advisable to leave . . . or . . . spaces between columns, dependent on the total . . . of the table.

14. The first column heading in block style should be typed at . . . . . . and the remaining column headings at . . . . . . set for each column.

15. To find starting point for horizontal line, press . . . . . . key and backspace . . .

16. The horizontal line ends at the . . . . . . and you should turn up . . . space before and . . . spaces after a horizontal line.

17. In standard punctuation a . . . . . . is required after initials but . . . full stop after the courtesy title Miss.

18. In standard punctuation a . . . is inserted at the end of each line at an address except the . . . line but there is . . . punctuation in Postcode.

19. Between surname and Esq. insert a . . . and a . . . in standard punctuation.

Turn to page 151 and check your answers. Score one point for each correct entry.
Total score: 50.

In exercises A, B and C, type each line or sentence three times. If time permits, complete your practice by typing each group of lines as it appears. Keep your eyes on the copy and return the carriage sharply.

Margins:
Elite 22—82
Pica 12—72

A. Review alphabet keys

1.   When all questions had been answered, an exclamation of joy broke out from the vast audience who had gathered around to listen to the popular quiz.

B. Build speed on word-family drill

2. day hay gay lay say pay way may did kid hid lid rid bid mid.

3. dine nine fine line mine pine wine lane sane wane vane pane.

4. The boy may have hid in the hay. Did he say she went today?

5. They may want wine when we dine at Pine Lodge in North Lane.

C. Improve control of word division

6. able, mail-able, read-able, suit-able, sens-ible, flex-ible.

7. so-cial, par-tial, ini-tial, finan-cial, spe-cial, pala-tial

8. pro-mote, pro-vided, per-mit, per-fume, pur-suit, pur-suant.

9. dis-may, dis-miss, dis-patch, dis-place, dis-grace, des-pair

Accuracy/speed practice   27 w.p.m.   Two minutes   Not more than two errors

A/S.30   You must not expect your friends to write to you if you | 11
do not write to them. This does not mean that you must send | 23
long letters - a note will do. Would not most of you rather | 35
have a note than no answer? Like us, you would want to know | 47
if your friends are well and happy. (S.I. 1.09) | 54

A/S.31   "If you want a garden," he said, "you will have to do a | 11
great deal of work, but in these days you can buy many tools | 23
which will be helpful for the heavy work, and thus save time | 35
and effort. You would not need to employ hired help, and so | 47
you would be able to save money." (S.I. 1.15) | 54

   1 | 2 | 3 | 4 | 5 | 6 | 7 | 8 | 9 | 10 | 11 | 12 |

Record your progress   Two minutes

R.14   There is still a very real risk of fire from oil stoves | 11
and lamps. A portable oil stove must have a firm base (with | 23
a guard around it) and it should always be placed out of the | 35
children's reach. Also, clothes left too near an oil stove, | 47
or gas fire, with no guard, might be set alight easily by a | 59
draught. (S.I. 1.16) | 60

   1 | 2 | 3 | 4 | 5 | 6 | 7 | 8 | 9 | 10 | 11 | 12 |

UNIT 51

Set out the following on a sheet of A4 paper. Use double spacing and side
headings.

LEASING OF MACHINERY

1st January 1977

l/c lease   LONG-TERM   to lease   At the end of the / period you may continue
the machine and the monthly leasing pay-
ment becomes the annual leasing payment.

l/by   Payment   All leases are normally paid/ Banker's
u/c   (caps)/   Order or by post office Giro or by cheque.

trs/le   Maintenance   The lease payments include maintenance
(caps)/   for the lease period originally quoted.

sk/   Accessories   Some
(caps)/   Certain accessories are supplied free of
charge. These will be stated on the
Lease Agreement.

Value Added Tax   VAT is chargeable on all charges
(caps)/   for machines leased.

Type the following on a sheet of A5 paper.

TRAVEL INSTRUCTIONS

Please read carefully the following notes:

1. Passports: travellers must hold valid passports,
    and a visa is necessary for certain countries.

2. Departure times: we reserve the right to alter
    departure times. Check with your local office
    24 hours before departure.

3. All timings are based on the 24-hour clock and in
    local time.

Example of 24-hour system

12.30 a.m.	0030
3.15 a.m.	0315
Noon	1200
2.10 p.m.	1410
9.20 p.m.	2120

Technique development

Letters with subject heading

When a letter has a subject heading, this should be typed as follows:

(a) Turn up two single-line spaces after salutation.

(b) In fully-blocked letters start the heading at left margin.

(c) Underscore the heading. No full stop should be typed after the last word unless this is an abbreviation.

(d) If there happens to be a final punctuation mark, do not underscore it.

1. Type the following letter in fully-blocked style on A4 paper (210 × 297 mm), using margins of Elite 22–82, Pica 12–72.

Ref EPH/MB

27 June 1977

A Wilkes & Sons Ltd
Hartfield Road
NORTHAMPTON   Northants
NN1 2HX

For the attention of the Buyer

Dear Sirs
                    (Turn up 2 single-line spaces)
Enquiry for Quotation
                    (Turn up 2 single-line spaces)
We have pleasure in referring to our Mr Richmond's call on Wednesday of last week, and, as requested, we attach our estimate for the woven material about which you enquired.

You will no doubt recall that the quality of the material previously purchased by you is a special weave, and, as prices have risen considerably since our last supply, we are taking the opportunity of quoting you for an alternative.

We hope that we can be of assistance to you in this respect, and await your further advice in due course.

Yours faithfully
J F PHILLIPS LTD

Joan Harper (Miss)
Outfitting Department

Enc

Type the following letter on A4 paper. Use suitable margins and insert heading
'RIGHTIME WATCHES'. Use standard punctuation.

Our Ref DC/AB

Today's date

Mrs T. Groves, 12 West Avenue, Rochester, Kent. ME1 1DZ

Dear Madam,

We recently became agents for RIGHTIME wrist watches, and, when next you are in town, we hope you will visit our store and see for yourself the good value we are offering. The following are only 3 of the wide price range:

Gold Plated   Expanding Bracelet   17 jewel   £15
Self-winding   Water-resistant   21 jewel   £23
Self-winding   Day and date   21 jewel   £18

These watches are all fitted with incabloc [INCABLOC] shock-protected fully-jewelled lever movement and guaranteed [GUARANTEED] for 2 years. From the enclosed brochure [BROCHURE] you will see that we offer a great variety of jewellery at reasonable prices.

Yrs. Ffly

S. COHEN & SONS

Douglas Carson
Manager

Job 17

Production Target—seven minutes

Type a copy of the following on A5 portrait paper. Use single spacing and
hanging paragraphs.

HIRE-PURCHASE

By this method / l.c.   Hire-purchase has now become a very important method of increasing sales. The customer pays a deposit when he receives the goods & then pays the balance owing by instalments, either

trs   monthly or weekly. Although the buyer can use the goods, it

these

must be remembered that ~~they~~ do not become his property until

N.P. / thus   the last payment has been made. [This method enables a person to

∂/# ⌢   ~~have the use of~~ use the gds for which he could not afford to pay

stet   the whole price ~~at once~~, but, of course, he will in the long run pay more than the actual cash price. Moreover, there is always a risk of his being perhaps persuaded to buy more than he can

>/   really afford / and so he would find it ~~impossible~~ *difficult* to keep up his payments.

2. Type the following letter on A4 paper, using margins of Elite 22—82, Pica 12—72 and fully-blocked style.

Ref HS/LE   28 September 1977

H A Ashworth & Co Ltd
28—30 Habberley Road
KIDDERMINSTER
Worcestershire   DY11 5PG

For the attention of Mr M Haynes

Dear Sirs

Order No 165/6

We refer to your order of 27 September, and enclose our confirmation.

We regret that, owing to unforeseen circumstances, we shall be unable to despatch the goods ordered before the end of next month. You will agree with us that it is not our practice to make delayed deliveries, and we apologize for the delay which is quite beyond our control.

Yours faithfully
MIDLAND FURNITURE CO LTD

H Smith
Sales Manager

Enc

3. Type the following letter on A4 paper (210 × 297 mm) in fully-blocked style. Use margins of Elite 25—80 Pica 15—70. Insert Our ref HS/TOM.

29 June 1977
Imperial Products Ltd   29 Jiggins Lane   Birmingham B32 3EL
For the attention of Mr G White
Dear Sirs
Enquiry ref J/H56
As requested in yr ltr of 26 June, we hv pleasure in enclosing our latest illustrated cat. wh contains details of our present prices & conditions of sale. We allow a cash disc. of 5% for payment within 7 days + 2½% for mthly settlements.
Yrs ffy Midland Furniture Co Ltd H Smith Sales Manager

Production typing

Job 13   Production Target—ten minutes

Display the following table on a sheet of A5 landscape paper. Use double spacing and rule by means of the underscore. Use block or centred method.

EUROPEAN COUNTRIES AND THEIR CAPITALS

Country	Capital	Country	Capital
Austria	Vienna	Hungary	Budapest
Belgium	Brussels	Italy	Rome
Denmark	Copenhagen	Norway	Oslo
Finland	Helsinki	Portugal	Lisbon
France	Paris	Spain	Madrid
Greece	Athens	Sweden	Stockholm
Holland	Amsterdam	Switzerland	Berne

Job 14   Production Target—eight minutes

Display the following on suitable paper

Caps and Underscore → Attention all gardeners
Consult us for
Lawn Turfing
Machine Digging
Landscaping
Fencing and Walling

Quotations on request

Caps → Prompt Service from
Al Gardeners Ltd
Derby Road, Kegworth, Derby

Job 15   Production Target—ten minutes

Address envelopes to the following, inserting courtesy titles where necessary. First with open punctuation. Then repeat with punctuation inserted.

James Emery   MD   43 Union Str   Glasgow   G1 4PG
Margaret Hatton   92 Dublin Rd   Belfast   N.I.   BT2 7HF
Robert Brown   56 George Street   Edinburgh   EH2 3NS
Hughes & Baxter   Solicitors   7 Fore Str   Exeter   Devon   EX4 3AT
Harris & Co. Ltd.   Heaton Rd   Newcastle upon Tyne   NE6 5QE
Mrs. J. Farwell   7 High Street   Leigh   Lancs   WN7 1BR
Wm. Lloyd   8 Court Rd   Reading   Berks RG7 4PW
Paul J Byrne   17 Kerry Road   Cork   Irish Republic

Technique development

Simple display in fully-blocked letters

Emphasis may be given to important facts in a letter by displaying these so that they catch the eye of the reader. Such displayed matter in fully-blocked letters starts at the left margin, one clear space being left above and below the displayed matter, as in the specimen below.

Practise typing fully-blocked letter with displayed matter

1. Type the following specimen letter on A4 paper (210 × 297 mm) in fully-blocked style, using margins of Elite 22–82, Pica 12–72. Open punctuation.

Ref JKL/GHJ

15 March 1977

J Barnes & Son Ltd
Park Road
HALESOWEN
West Midlands   B63 4BB

For the attention of Mail Order Department

Dear Sirs

Please send me as soon as possible to the above address the goods listed below:
        (Turn up 2 single-line spaces)
12 pairs Nylon Sheets, Style H232, @ £1.75 each
12 Quilted Bedspreads, Style H128, @ £3.50 each
        (Turn up 2 single-line spaces)
All to be in size 3' 0" (76 mm), colour pink.

We enclose cheque for £63.80 which includes 80p for postage.

Yours faithfully
G & H INGRAM LTD

J K Lambert
Stores Manager

Enc

Note use of apostrophe for feet and double quotation marks for inches. If these signs are used, no space is left between the figure and the sign but one space is left after the sign

Column display in fully-blocked letters

When matter is to be displayed in columns in the body of a fully-blocked letter, you should take the following steps to ensure that three spaces are left between the longest line of one column and the start of the next column.

(a) Starting at the left-hand margin, tap space bar once for each character and space in the longest line of the first column plus three extra spaces for spacing between the first and second column.

(b) Set a tab stop at point reached.

(c) Starting from tab stop, tap space bar once for each character and space in the longest line of the second column plus 3 extra spaces for the spacing between the second and third columns.

(d) Set a tab stop at point reached.

(e) Repeat (c) and (d) for any additional columns.

Technique development

Ruling

A neat and pleasing appearance may be given to column work by ruling in ink or by the use of the underscore.

An *'open'* table has no ruled lines (like the column work you have been doing). Its main use is for displayed columns of items in the body of a letter.

A *'ruled'* table has the column headings separated from the column items by horizontal lines above and below the headings, and below the last line in the table.

When typing a *'ruled'* table proceed as follows:

(a) Find vertical starting point by calculating number of typed lines and spaces—remember to count the horizontal lines.

(b) In the usual way back-space to find left margin. Set margin and tab stops.

(c) From last tab stop, tap space bar once for each character and space in the longest line of the last column *plus two extra spaces* and set right-hand margin at point reached.

(d) Type main heading at left margin if block style is used, or centre if centred style. Turn up three single spaces and return carriage to left margin.

(e) Press margin release key and backspace two. This gives you the starting point for the horizontal line which is typed by means of the underscore and finishes at the right margin.

Note: After the first horizontal line, remember to turn up *twice after* and *once before* a horizontal line.

Practise typing 'ruled' table

1. After studying the above instructions, type the following table on A5 portrait paper (148 × 210 mm), typing the body in double spacing. Leave three spaces between columns and centre the whole table horizontally and vertically. Use block or centred style. Rule by underscore. (The instructions at the side of the table are given as a guide.)

TURN UP
3 spaces
2 spaces

1 space
2 spaces

NOTE: If column headings are centred the scale-points will be:
Col. 1 18 (12)
  ,, 2 35 (29)
  ,, 3 49 (43)

PROPERTY FOR SALE
_____

Type	Town	County
Coaching Inn	Arundel	West Sussex
Guest House	Eastbourne	East Sussex
Hotel	Christchurch	Dorset
Thatched Cottage	Clevedon	Avon
Family Business	Bridgend	Mid Glamorgan

2. Type the following table on A5 portrait paper (148 × 210 mm) in double spacing. Leave three spaces between columns and centre the table horizontally and vertically. Use block or centred style. Rule lines by means of underscore.

SOME POST TOWNS WITH NEW AND OLD COUNTIES
_____

Post Town	New County	Old County
Aberystwyth	Dyfed	Cardiganshire
Barmouth	Gwynedd	Merioneth
Bilston	West Midlands	Staffordshire
Birkenhead	Merseyside	Cheshire
Bradford	West Yorkshire	Yorkshire
Dudley	West Midlands	Worcestershire

Further exercises in column work with horizontal ruling are given on page 32 of **Practical Typing Exercises, Book One**

2. Type the following letter on A4 paper (210 × 297 mm) in fully-blocked style, using margins of Elite 22–82, Pica 12–72. Open punctuation.

Our Ref PEW/PG   6 October 1977

Horizon Publishers Ltd
Croesyceiliog
Cwmbran
Gwent   NP4 2XF

For the attention of P Kirkhouse Esq

Dear Sirs

Christmas Annuals

We have today received your latest catalogue and would like
to place the following order for children's Annuals:

12 only   TREASURE HUNTING   £1.20 each
10 only   SOCCER STARS   £1.10 each
15 only   POP IDOLS   £1.75 each

As we shall be putting our Christmas display on show in
2 weeks' time, please deliver this order by 18 October.

Yours faithfully
EDUCATIONAL BOOKS LTD

P E WEDGE
PURCHASING OFFICER

Note: Display as instructed on page 70

3. Type the following letter on A4 paper in fully-blocked style, using margins of Elite 20–85, Pica 10–75. Abbreviations to be typed in full where necessary.

Our Ref KB/JB

9 July 1977

Miss M J Field 20 Bath Road Bitton Bristol BS15 6HB

Dear Madam

As requested in yr ltr of 7 July 1977, we hv pleasure in
sending you under separate cover specimen copies of the
books of wh you ask, as follows:

Study notes on Commerce   J A C Shafto   £3.00
Office Practice, Book 1   M Watcham   £1.30
Secretarial Dictation   Sharp + Crozier   £0.95

We trust tt you wl find these of help to you & look
fwd to the rect of yr order in due course.

Yrs ffy   McGraw-Hill Book Company (UK) Limited
Business Education Department

When the heading is SHORTER than the LONGEST COLUMN ITEM, and the centred style is used, the HEADING must be centred over the longest item in the column as follows:

(a) i Find the centre point of the column by tapping space bar once for every two letters or spaces in the longest column item, beginning from the point set for the start of the column. This will bring the printing point to the centre of the column.

ii From this centre point back-space once for every two letters or spaces in the heading. Type the heading from the point reached.

(b) The column items will start at the point already set for the start of the column. If block style is used, both column headings and column items are blocked, as in Exercise 1 on page 97.

Practise centring headings *over column items*

3. On A5 landscape paper (210 × 148 mm) type the following table in double spacing, leaving three spaces between columns. Centre the table horizontally and vertically. Also centre main heading and column headings over column items.

EXAMINATION RESULTS

Name	Shorthand	Typing	Commerce
Alice Carter	Passed	Passed	Passed
John Brown	Distinction	Not Passed	Not Passed
Edna Williams	Passed	Distinction	Distinction
Rose Davies	Not Passed	Passed	Passed

4. Type the following on A5 landscape paper (210 × 148 mm) in double spacing, leaving three spaces between columns. Centre the table horizontally and vertically.

GENERAL GUIDE TO OVEN TEMPERATURE

Slow	Moderately Hot	Hot	Very Hot
Egg Dishes	Custard	Bread	Puff Pastry
Meringues	Biscuits	Baked Fish	Scones
Oven Stews	Cheese	Small Cakes	Flaky Pastry
Milk Puddings	Sponges	Sandwich Cakes	Yorkshire Pudding

5. Type the following on A5 landscape paper (210 × 148 mm) in double spacing leaving three spaces between columns. Centre the table horizontally and vertically.

METRIC UNITS FOR CERTAIN COMMODITIES

metre (m)	centimetre (cm)	millimetre (mm)	kilograms (kg) or grams (g)
Fabric length	~~Fabric~~ *Clothing*	~~Hardware~~ *Lawn Mowers*	Butter
Carpet width	~~Blankets~~ *Fabric Width*	Kitchen Units	Tea
Carpet length	~~Sheets~~ *Blankets*	Shoes	Sugar
Stet Timber ~~length~~ *width*	~~Clothing~~ *Sheets*	~~Lawn Mowers~~ *Hardware*	Chocolates

Further exercises on column headings are given on page 31 of **Practical Typing Exercises, Book One**

Type each exercise (A, B and C) three times. Keep your eyes on the copy and return the carriage sharply.

Margins:
Elite 22—82
Pica 12—72

A. Review alphabet keys

1.   The big swarthy cyclist, who was known as Jacko, seemed quite relaxed when he received first prize at the end of the arduous ride through the snow and ice of the mountain.

B. Improve control of shift key

2. Frank Jones Denis Kelly Stock Louis Aston Roger Yates Epping

3. Frank Jones and Denis Kelly went to the West Indies in July.

4. Louis Stock and Nancy Ball visited Epping Forest last April.

5. Roger Yates joined the Aston Villa Football Club on 1 March.

C. Review hyphen key

6. p-p; p-p; 2-9, 3-8, 4-7, 5-6, con- com- mis- pre- for- dis-.

7. Full-time, up-to-date, blue-grey, 48-page, re-cover, co-opt.

8. Full-time students wore pin-striped blue-grey ties. He con- sidered that the up-to-date 48-page document was now ready.

Accuracy/speed practice   28 w.p.m.   One minute   Not more than one error

A/S.32   Each year there are new typewriters on the market, and   11
you must know about them so that you are up to date when you   23
wish to move to a new job. **(S.I. 1.14)**   28

A/S.33   A computer is now being made that will store voice pat-   11
terns. It will know your voice when you speak to it, and it   23
will answer your queries. **(S.I. 1.21)**   28

A/S.34   Will this computer mean that you, as a typist, will not   11
be needed? Not in your life-time. It will take many years   23
before it is ready for use. **(S.I. 1.25)**   28

    1 | 2 | 3 | 4 | 5 | 6 | 7 | 8 | 9 | 10 | 11 | 12 |

Record your Progress   One minute

R.15   For many years we have been specialists in all kinds of   11
fitted carpets - all of our selling and fitting staff having   23
spent their whole lives in this trade. All our work is done   35
by expert craftsmen. **(S.I. 1.26)**   39

    1 | 2 | 3 | 4 | 5 | 6 | 7 | 8 | 9 | 10 | 11 | 12 |

UNIT 54

Technique development

Tabulation

Typing column headings—block style

In addition to the main heading of a table, each column may have a heading. The length of the column heading must be taken into account when deciding which is the longest line in each column. When there are headings above columns, proceed as follows:
(a) Find longest line in each column. It could be the heading or a column item.

(b) Back-space as usual to find left margin, remembering to take into account the spacing between columns, and set left margin and tab stops. Column headings **and** column items start at the left margin and at the tab stops set for the longest line of each column.

Practise typing column work with blocked headings

1. Using A5 portrait paper (148 × 210 mm) type the following table in double spacing, leaving three spaces between columns.

UNITS OF MEASUREMENT IN METRICATION

Millimetre (mm)	Centimetre (cm)	Kilograms (kg)
Baths	Blankets	Cement
Cookers	Clothing	Fertilizers
Roof tiles	Fabrics	Mortar
Sink units	Pillow cases	Plaster
Wall heaters	Sheets	Putty

Typing column headings—centred style

The main heading is centred, and if the COLUMN heading is the LONGEST LINE (as in Exercise 1 above), the COLUMN ITEMS are centred under it as follows.
(a) Find the centre point of the column by tapping space bar once for every two letters or spaces in the heading. This will bring the carriage to the centre point of the heading.

(b) From the centre point back-space in the usual way once for every two letters or spaces in the longest line under this heading. This gives you the starting point for each item in the column.
(c) After typing the heading, re-set tab stops to the scale-points for column items where necessary.

Practise centring column items *under column headings*

2. Using A5 portrait paper (148 × 210 mm) type the following table in double spacing, leaving three spaces between columns. Centre the main heading and centre the column items under column headings.

FOOD PRODUCTS

Vegetables	Meat and Poultry	Fresh Fruit
Beans	Lamb	Apples
Cabbage	Pork	Apricots
Celery	Veal	Bananas
Peas	Chicken	Peaches
Sprouts	Duck	Pineapple

UNIT 69

Carbon copies

All business firms keep an exact copy of letters, invoices, and other documents they send out. For this purpose the typist uses *carbon paper*. To take a carbon copy—

(a) Place face downwards on flat surface the sheet on which typing is to be done.

(b) On top of this, with coated (shiny) surface *upwards*, place a sheet of carbon paper.

(c) Place on top of these the sheet of paper on which carbon copy is to be made. If additional copies are required, repeat steps (b) and (c).

(d) Pick up all sheets together and insert into machine with coated surface of carbon paper facing platen.

(e) Make sure that feed rolls grip all sheets at the same time.

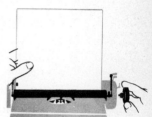

Carbon paper has a dull side and a glossy side. The glossy side does the work.

Glossy paper is put against the paper on which the copy is to be made.

You always have one more sheet of typing paper than of carbon paper.

Straighten sides and top of pack carefully before inserting it in your machine.

Hold pack with left hand; turn cylinder smoothly with right hand.

Erasing with carbon copies

If you have to make an erasure when taking carbon copies, *before* erasing insert a strip of *thickish* paper between the shiny side of your carbon paper and the carbon copy. Then erase the error on the top copy. Remove strip of paper and erase error on carbon copy.

If you are taking more than one carbon copy, insert strip of paper *behind* shiny surface of *each sheet* of carbon paper. Erase on top and all carbon copies. Then return carriage to writing point and type correct letter or letters.

NOTE: You must *never* overtype, i.e., alter an error by typing one letter over another.

1. Type the following letter on A4 paper (210 × 297 mm) using margins of Elite 22–82, Pica 12–72. Take a carbon copy. [= new paragraph.

Our Ref LW/CC 28 May 1977 R W York Esq MA BSc JP
Principal Doone Comprehensive School North Road Poole Dorset BH14 OLS
Dear Mr York In July we shall have a vacancy for a school leaver, aged between 16 and 17, in our Internal Audit Department. Applicants must have a minimum of 4 'O' Levels, 2 of which should be English and Maths. [The post offers an excellent opportunity to a person who intends to follow an accountancy career, and day-release facilities will be available. [I am enclosing 4 application forms and should be pleased if you would be kind enough to let your pupils know of this vacancy. Completed application forms should be returned to me.
Yours sincerely L Watson Personnel Officer

Skill building

Type each exercise (A, B and C) three times. Keep your eyes on the copy and return the carriage sharply.

Margins:
Elite 22—82
Pica 12—72

A. Review alphabet keys

1. If she makes a determined and real effort, we are quite sure she will very quickly be enjoying a high place with the experts, and may win a valuable prize.

B. Improve control of figure keys

2. wee 233 our 974 try 546 ere 343 wit 285 ire 843 too 599 678.

3. 330 339 338 337 336 992 993 994 995 123 456 789 101 293 234.

4. Final 7%, payable 3rd August, making 12½%. Profit £456,890.

5. Flight 417 leaves at 1350, while Flight 1482 leaves at 1619.

C. Build accuracy on common suffix drill

6. using ending asking making turning morning replying advising

7. comment shipment equipment settlement adjustment arrangement

8. We will not comment about the shipments of equipment to you.

9. In the morning we shall be asking him what car he is taking.

Accuracy/speed practice   30 w.p.m.   Two minutes   Not more than two errors

A/S.47
Some large offices have a pool of typists who share the	11
work to be done, but we do not know whether or not this is a	23
good plan. This is a matter which must be left to each firm	35
to decide, based on the amount of work which has to be done,	47
and on the staff employed. You may like working in a typing	59
pool. (S.I. 1.17)	60

A/S.48
With the keen competition which we have to face both at	11
home and abroad, we must do our best to bring up to date all	23
our equipment. It is only by doing so that we shall be able	35
to increase our output, and so reduce our costs. In my view	47
it is essential to decide here and now on the best course to	59
take. (S.I. 1.25)	60

1 | 2 | 3 | 4 | 5 | 6 | 7 | 8 | 9 | 10 | 11 | 12 |

Record your progress   Two minutes

R.21
Since the beginning of the year we have employed about	11
275 more men than ever before, and 340 more than last year.	23
Under our new profit scheme we should like to pay 5% to the	34
workmen and 5% to the staff, and we shall require at least	46
£10,000 extra to enable us to do so. Your Board proposes to	58
add another £15,000 to the reserve fund, bringing it up to	69
£275,000. (S.I. 1.27)	71

1 | 2 | 3 | 4 | 5 | 6 | 7 | 8 | 9 | 10 | 11 | 12 |

UNIT 68

2. Type the following letter on A4 paper (210 × 297 mm), using margins of Elite 22—82, Pica 12—72. Take a carbon copy. All abbreviations to be typed in full.

Ref. ARM/JAY

5th April 1977

H. J. Manson Ltd
Woodland Road
Leominster, Herefordshire, HR6 8JJ

For the atten of Mr A Green

Dear Sirs

Non-delivery of Goods

We hv recd yr ltr of 3 April 1977 concerning the non-delivery by the rlywy co. of the gds sent to you 2 wks ago.

We hv made enquiries in our Despatch Dept to find that these gds were handed to the rlwy co's carrier, who signed for the rect of the gds wh were securely packed & correctly labelled, & we are surprised to learn th the consignment has not yet arrived.

We hv taken the matter up w the rlwy co as per the enclosed copy of letter, & as soon as we hear anything definite, we wl advise you.

Yrs ffy

MIDLAND FURNITURE CO. LTD

A. R. MILLER
MANAGER
Enc.

Numbered or lettered paragraphs or items

Paragraphs are sometimes numbered or lettered as follows. The numbers or letters may be followed by a full stop or placed in brackets. If a full stop is used, leave two spaces after the full stop. If brackets are used, also leave two spaces after closing bracket, as in examples below.

```
1.  Surname        1)  Surname        (a)  Surname
2.  Christian name  2)  Christian name  (b)  Christian name
```

Practise typing numbered paragraphs

3. Type the following on A5 landscape paper (210 mm × 148 mm) in double spacing, using margins of Elite 22—82, Pica 12—72. Take a carbon copy.

CHARGES

The payment of £35.00 covers the following, inclusive of VAT:

```
1.  All lectures
2.  Accommodation
3.  Morning coffee and all main meals from Tuesday morning
    until Saturday evening
4.  Dinner/Dance on Friday evening
5.  Visit to theatre (details to be given later)
```

Further exercises on enumeration are given on pages 10 and 23 of **Practical Typing Exercises, Book One**

UNIT 55

2. Following the instructions given on page 94, type the following table on A5 landscape paper (210 × 148 mm). Use double-line spacing and leave three spaces between columns. Main heading should be typed on the 13th single-line space from the top edge of paper. Block or centre the main heading.

DIFFICULT SPELLING

argument	accommodation	forfeit
omission	committed	rhythm
forcibly	occurred	separately
benefited	believe	definite

3. Type the following table on A5 landscape paper (210 × 148 mm), using double-line spacing. Type main heading on 13th single-line space from top edge of paper. Leave three spaces between columns. Block or centre the main heading.

NORTH SEA OIL FIELDS

Andrew	Cormorant	Maureen
Beryl	Crawford	Ninian
Brae	Forties	Piper
Brent	Heather	Tern
Bruce	Hutton	Thistle

Vertical centring

The proper vertical arrangement of columns will add greatly to the effectiveness of your display. Use the same method as for vertical display (see page 37).

Practise vertical and horizontal display

4. Type the following table on A5 landscape paper (210 × 148 mm) in double-line spacing. Centre vertically and horizontally and leave three spaces between columns. Block or centre the main heading. The details below the table are given as a guide for the vertical centring.

SOME TOWNS NOT REQUIRING COUNTY IF POSTCODE IS USED

Bath	Cardiff	Inverness	Shrewsbury
Belfast	Carlisle	Leeds	Sunderland
Birmingham	Dundee	Liverpool	Swansea
Bournemouth	Edinburgh	Londonderry	Warrington
Brighton	Huddersfield	Newcastle-upon-Tyne	Wolverhampton
Bristol	Hull	Sheffield	York

Vertical display

Number of vertical line-spaces on A5 landscape paper	= 35	Difference to be divided between top and bottom margins 35 − 14	= 21
Number of vertical lines and spaces in table	= 14	Divide by 2 (ignore fraction)	= 10
		Begin typing heading on next line	= 11

Further exercises on Vertical Display are given on page 30 of **Practical Typing Exercises, Book One**

Skill Building

In exercises A, B and C, type each line or sentence three times. If time permits, complete your practice by typing each group of lines as it appears. Keep your eyes on the copy and return the carriage sharply.

Margins:
Elite 22—82
Pica 12—72

A. Review alphabet keys

1.　　　　If he makes a determined and zealous effort, I am quite sure Robert will very quickly join the top-ranking experts.

B. Improve skill on fluency drill

2. she her his him are not has had any our who did but was see.

3. they that week know time will days this here your food when.

4. They know that this food must have been left here some days.

5. Your team hope that they will have much more time this week.

C. Build speed on phrases

6. to me, to go, to do, if it, if he, if we, do we, do it, out.

7. and the, for the, may the, can the, you are, you can, it is.

8. If you are late, you can get the last train to go from town.

9. If he calls, do we want him to do the work for the firm now?

Accuracy/speed practice　　　28 w.p.m.　Two minutes　　　Not more than two errors

A/S.35　　　　I wish you could see and try out our new car. It is as　　**11**
smooth and as swift as a cloud. I am sure you will like it　　**23**
and will want to drive it when we go on holiday to Scotland.　　**35**
I think we should leave here about 0700 hours, and that will　　**47**
get us on to the M6 before the city rush hour. (S.I. 1.11)　　**56**

A/S. 36　　　　When you eat your Brazil nuts at Christmas, do you ever　　**11**
think of the men who pick them, and the risks they run to do　　**23**
so? One of the risks is the falling of nuts from the trees,　　**35**
which grow to a great height. What we usually call nuts are　　**47**
not nuts at all - they are, in fact, the seeds. (S.I. 1.12)　　**56**

　　1 | 2 | 3 | 4 | 5 | 6 | 7 | 8 | 9 | 10 | 11 | 12 |

Record your progress　　　　　　　　　　　　　　　　Two minutes

R.16　　　　It may help to give the new cash gains (they are listed　　**11**
in Rule 99) which apply as from 1 August 1977, to all staff　　**23**
who have given 12 months' service in the firm.　　**32**

　　　　A grant of £50 will be made in the case of an injury in　　**43**
the course of duty - a claim must be made within 4 months of　　**55**
the date on which the injury occurred. Make claims on form　　**67**
216/C. (S.I. 1.16)　　**68**

　　1 | 2 | 3 | 4 | 5 | 6 | 7 | 8 | 9 | 10 | 11 | 12 |

UNIT 56　　　　　　　　　　　　　　　　　　　　　　　　　　75

Technique development

Tabulation

Arrangement of items in columns

You may be required to arrange items in column form in such a way that they are horizontally centred on the page, with equal spaces between the columns and with equal margins. This can easily be done by means of the back-spacing method you have already used for the centring of headings.

A. Horizontal centring of columns with main heading blocked

1. *Preliminary Steps*
(a) Clear all tab stops (refer to Page 32).
(b) Clear margin stops by bringing them to the extreme ends of the margin scale.
(c) Insert paper, seeing that the left edge is at 0 on the carriage-position scale.
(d) Bring carriage to centre point of paper (refer to Page 35).
Set *1st tab stop* at this point for the start of the second column

2. *Steps to determine starting point for each column*
(a) Back-space once for every two letters and spaces in the longest item of each column, saying them to yourself in pairs. If there is an odd letter in any column, carry this on to the next column.
(b) Back-space once for every two spaces to be left between the columns, carrying on to next column any space left over.
(c) Set *left margin stop* at the point thus reached.
(d) Starting from this margin, tap space bar once for each letter and space in the longest line of the first column and once for each blank space between first and second columns.

(e) Starting from this 1st tab stop, again tap space bar once for each letter and space in the longest item of the second column and for each blank space between second and third columns.
Set *2nd tab stop* at this point for the start of the third column.
Continue in the same way for any additional columns.
(f) Tap space bar for final column and check that the two margins are equal.

3. *Typing the table*
(a) Type main heading at left margin. Turn up three single line spaces.
(b) Bring carriage to left margin and type first item in first column.
(c) Tabulate to second column and type first item. Then tabulate to each of the remaining columns and type the first item.
(d) Continue in the same way with the rest of the table.
NOTE: It is essential that you complete each horizontal line before starting the next.

B. Horizontal centring of columns with main heading centred

Follow the steps given in Nos. 1, 2 and 3 above, but centre the main heading in the full width of the paper instead of blocking it at the left margin.

Practise column display typing

1. Carrying out the instructions given above, type the following table on A5 landscape paper (210 × 148 mm). Start the heading on the 13th single-line space from top of paper and type it either at the left margin as instructed in A. above or centre as in B. Turn up three single-line spaces after the heading. Use double spacing for body and leave three spaces between columns. Scale-points for start of columns are given as a guide. Those in brackets are for pica type.

<u>PERSONAL QUALITIES</u>

30 (21)	45 (36)	58 (49)
Accuracy	Courtesy	Pleasantness
Alertness	Initiative	Punctuality
Ambition	Loyalty	Reliability
Common Sense	Neatness	Tact

Note: If the main heading is centred this should start at scale-points: Elite 41, Pica 32.

Sizes of envelopes

C5 229 × 162 mm (9" × 6⅜")
takes A5 paper unfolded
and A4 paper folded once

C6 162 × 114 mm (6⅜" × 4½")
takes A4 paper folded twice
and A5 paper folded once

D11 220 × 110 mm (8⅝" × 4¼")
takes A4 paper folded equally into three

Post Office regulations

1. Post Office regulations require address to be parallel to the length and not to the breadth of the envelope.

2. Post town should preferably be typed in capitals.

3. The *Postcode* should be typed as follows:

(a) It is always the last item in the address and should have a line to itself.

(b) If it is impossible, because of lack of space, to put the code on a separate line, type it *six* spaces to the right of the last line.

(c) Always type code in block capitals.

(d) Do not use full stops or any punctuation marks between or after the characters in the code.

(e) Leave *one* clear space between the two halves of the code.

(f) *Never* underline the code.

Example:
Block Style—open punctuation

Messrs W H Ramsay & Co
Mortimer Street
LONDON
W1N 8BA

For further information
see Post Office Guide

Skill building

In exercises A, B and C, type each line or sentence three times. If time permits, complete your practice by typing each group of lines as it appears. Keep your eyes on the copy and return the carriage sharply.

A.   Review alphabet keys

1.   As the young musician, who wore a jacket of vivid blue, strolled slowly round the piazza, the quaint sounds from his guitar and his relaxed manner reflected the evening calm.

B.   Improve control of shift key

2. Ben More, Great Yarmouth, New Haven, Victoria Road, Cheddar.

3. Kingston St. Mary, Port Talbot, Jedburgh, Upton, Iver, Stow.

4. Great Yarmouth is in Norfolk; Kingston St. Mary in Somerset.

5. New Haven, Conn., U.S.A. Upton-upon-Severn, Worcestershire.

C.   Speed up control of space bar

6. For the two old men, the new day will be one of fun and joy.

7. We will go to the park in time to see the start of the game.

8. One of the best ways to gain speed is to type easy material.

9. He is on the way. I am to go to the boat in that bay. Yes.

Accuracy/speed practice   30 w.p.m.   1½ minutes   Not more than one error

A/S.45   You will be very glad to know that we can now make more | 11
machines this year than last year, and we can make all vital | 23
spare parts. During the next 3 months we shall not need any | 35
orders as we are going to produce a new model soon. (S.I. 1.20) | 45

A/S.46   There is nothing that annoys a business man more than a | 11
clerk who forgets to do the jobs given to him. An excellent | 23
plan is to have a pad on your desk, so that you can jot down | 35
straight away anything that you are required to do. (S.I. 1.24) | 45

    1 | 2 | 3 | 4 | 5 | 6 | 7 | 8 | 9 | 10 | 11 | 12 |

Record your progress   1½ minutes

R.20   We have had your name on our books for some months now, | 11
but although we have, from time to time, sent you details of | 23
properties, we have not heard from you. If you still desire | 35
to buy a country residence, please complete and return to us | 47
the attached form, so that we may know what the position is. | 59
                            (S.I. 1.22)

    1 | 2 | 3 | 4 | 5 | 6 | 7 | 8 | 9 | 10 | 11 | 12 |

UNIT 66

93

Addressing of envelopes, postcards, etc.

1. Always be sure to use an envelope sufficiently large to take the letter and any enclosures.
2. Many firms have their name and address printed in the top left corner. This ensures the safe and speedy return of the letter if, for any reason, it cannot be delivered.
3. Always type the envelope for each letter immediately after typing the letter.
4. Remember to type the envelopes for any extra carbon copies which may be sent to other offices or persons for their information.
5. Special instructions, such as Personal, Confidential Private, should be typed, in capitals and underscored, two spaces above the name of the addressee.
6. Single-line space and block style are preferable on a small envelope. With larger envelopes the address may be better displayed and more easily read by being typed in double-line spacing.
7. On most envelopes the address should be started about 50 mm from the left-hand edge and the first line should be approximately half-way down.

Forms of Address—open punctuation

Block style—Begin each line at the same point on the scale.
Open punctuation—No punctuation after abbreviations or at the end of a line. Leave *one* clear space before and after each initial in a person's name. Mr (space) J (space) R (space) Browning

```
Mr J R Browning
21 North Drive
Hamble
SOUTHAMPTON
SO3 5HA
```

Degrees and qualifications—No punctuation. No space between letters representing a degree or qualification, but one clear space between each group of letters. Mr (space) F (space) Eastwood (space) MA (space) BSc

```
Mr F Eastwood MA BSc
```

Courtesy title
1. Must always be used with a person's name—
   Miss M K Green   J Bishop Esq   Mr W P Stevens
   Mrs G Hill
   (If you are not sure whether a lady is Mrs or Miss, use the abbreviation Ms without a full stop)
2. When writing to a male correspondent, you may use Mr OR Esq but NEVER both. REV replaces Mr or Esq—Rev R S Smith
3. Partnerships—The word MESSRS is used before the name of a partnership—Messrs Martin & Sons Messrs Johnson & Co   Messrs Bowron & Jones
4. *No* courtesy title used in the following cases
   (a) Before the name of a limited company—
       P Yates & Co Ltd   W Robertson & Sons Ltd
       Carter & Bailey Ltd
   (b) With impersonal names—The British Non-Ferrous Metal Co
   (c) When a title is included in a name—
       Sir John Brown & Co   Sir Arthur Hamilton-Grey

Practise envelope-addressing

Type the following addresses in block style. Insert any courtesy titles that have been omitted. Open punctuation. Type post towns in capitals.

```
W R Wiseman Esq  20 Northbrook Road  Brighton  BN1 1NP

W J James & Sons   25—29 Doncaster Road   Scunthorpe

South Humberside   DN15 7AA

F L Booth & Co Ltd  Durham Road  Sunderland  SR3 4AQ

W Willis & Son  West Street  Billingham  Cleveland  TS23 2DB

Smith & Jones   40 Clapgates Road  Warrington  WA5 5AD

Miss M Wiseman  BA  64 Russell Road  Fishponds  Bristol  BS16 3HD

The Cresswell Engineering Co  Bridge Road  Luton  Bedfordshire

LU1 0RW

Rev H A Field  4 Hunt Road  Liverpool  L3 9EG
```

Further exercises on envelope-addressing are given on pages 18 and 38 of **Practical Typing Exercises, Book One**

Typing postcards

Many firms send postcards (A6–148 × 105 mm) in acknowledgment of letters and orders. The name and address of the firm sending the card are usually printed across the top of the card. These formal acknowledgments are typed like memos with no salutation and no complimentary close.

Note the following points:

(a) Centre and type firm's name and address, starting four spaces from top of card.
(b) Use margins of five spaces on either side.
(c) Always use single spacing with double between paragraphs. Paragraphs may be indented or blocked.
(d) After typing address turn up three single spaces and at left-hand margin insert the reference. On the same line, back-space from right-hand margin and type date.
(e) Turn up two single spaces and type body.

Practise typing postcards

1. Following the above instructions and using postcard size paper (148 × 105 mm) type the following postcard. On the reverse side, address the postcard to yourself.

```
                    RAYMOND DRESSES LTD.
          59 Bryanston Street, London.   W1A 2AZ



BMT/FL                                    Today's date

Thank you for your order No. B/Sep/29 dated (insert
date).

The various sizes of winter dresses you require
are being sent by passenger train by Friday next,
(insert date).
```

2. Using postcard size paper, type the following. Address it on the reverse side ready for despatch.

```
To: I. C. MacLean & Sons,      From: B. B. Manson & Co. Ltd.,
    Commercial Quay,                 West Road,
    Aberdeen.   AB2 3HE              Newcastle-upon-Tyne.   NE5 2BJ
```

(Insert suitable date)

```
We have received your letter dated (insert date) , and have
telephoned the railway company, who have promised to trace
the packages despatched from our warehouse on (insert date)  .
As soon as we have further news as to their whereabouts we
will telephone you.
```

Consolidation

Production typing

Job 7   Production Target—fifteen minutes

Type the following letter on A4 paper, ready for signature, taking a carbon copy. Use a suitable date and mark the letter for the attention of Miss S. Shemming. Address an envelope. Set margins at Elite 22–82, Pica 12–72. The square bracket [means that you start a new paragraph.

Ref IES/HW

Messrs Bradley & Sons   5 Clarence Parade   Southsea   Hants   PO5 3NW

Dear Sirs

CLEANERS & POLISHERS

With ref to our reps call on 14 October, when you enquired abt prices for our new Cleaners & Polishers, we hv pleasure in quoting you as follows:

Junior model   £15.20   (Typist: please leave 3 spaces between the 2 columns)

Junior de luxe model   £17.60

Extra Super model   £21.75

The above prices do not include VAT. [We enclose a copy of our latest cat in wh you wl find illustrations of the models in question. [If there is any further information you wd like to hv, please do not hesitate to communicate w us.

Yrs ffy   J W Bright & Sons   Sales Manager

Job 8   Production Target—eight minutes

Display the following on a sheet of A5 landscape paper. Centre each line horizontally and the whole vertically. For vertical spacing, follow the instructions at the right-hand side of the notice.

IT'S A SUPER SALE

Massive range of toys and games
Books to suit all ages   In double
Stationery for all purposes   spacing
Glassware of all descriptions
Cut-price records

                 Leave 2 clear

Hurry to our Sale on   Leave 1 clear

Tuesday, 11 November   Leave 2 clear

FANCY GOODS LTD
Bell Street   Single spacing
DUNDEE

3. Type the following letter in fully-blocked style, using standard punctuation. Use A4 paper and single-line spacing. Margins: Elite 22–82, Pica 12–72. Type an envelope.

Our Ref. JTF/DAN

10th June, 1977

Messrs. W. J. Southall & Sons,
St. Helen's Crescent,
CROYDON,
Surrey.   CR9 6BA

<u>For the attention of J. T. Firth, Esq.</u>

Dear Sirs,

TRIAL ORDER

Thank you for your letter dated 6th June and for your current leaflet.

We shall be glad if you will forward immediately one each of the 2 articles illustrated, viz.:

1 Child's Chair No. 7103 @ £15.75
1 Linen Basket No. 1428B @ £13.20

We enclose cheque for £28.95 in payment, and rely on you not to fail to make prompt despatch, as both items are required by 22nd June.

Yours faithfully,
BARCLAY, TURNBULL & CO. LTD.

J. T. Firth
Sales Manager.

Encl.

Note: When using standard punctuation, 'st', 'nd', 'rd', 'th' may be used in dates. Similarly, a comma may follow the month.

Steps in typing a business letter

(a) Insert paper into machine.

(b) Estimate approximate number of words in body of letter.

(c) Set appropriate spacing and margins.

(d) Type reference and date, and inside address and salutation. Check for errors.

(e) Type body of letter. Ensure even right margin. Check for errors.

(f) Type complimentary closing and signature. Check for errors.

N.B. Always final check your work before *taking paper out of machine.*

Further exercises on fully-blocked letters with standard punctuation are given on pages 4–9 of **Practical Typing Exercises, Book One**

Type the following on a sheet of A5 portrait paper and take a carbon copy. Set margins at Elite 12–62, Pica 5–55. Use single spacing with double spacing between paragraphs. Centre heading on the typing line, and use indented paragraphs.

<u>METRIC MEASUREMENTS</u>

When typing metric measurements, pay particular attention to the following:

(a) <u>Never</u> add an 's' to the symbol to form the plural - symbols are the same in the plural as they are in the singular, e.g., 20 metres - 20 m.

(b) <u>Never</u> put a full stop after a symbol unless it occurs at the end of a sentence.

(c) <u>Always</u> leave a space between the figure(s) and the symbol, e.g., 20 (space) m.

(d) Most symbols are small letters, but there are a few in upper case, such as C and M which stand for Celsius and Mega. Certain keyboards (teleprinters for example) have upper case letters only, and when using such machines the unit should be typed in full, e.g., 15 MILLIMETRES.

(e) At line ends <u>never</u> separate the figure(s) from the symbol.

(f) The symbol l (small L) should not be used for litre - write the word in full.

Address envelopes to the following. Insert any necessary courtesy titles, and remember to type post town in capitals.

P Wilkes & Sons Ltd   45 Grosvenor Hill   London W1X 4ER

Miss M Coxon   16 Bromley Lane   Chislehurst   Kent   BR7 6LM

Allan Owen BCom   58 West Road   Newcastle-upon-Tyne   NE5 2BJ

Johnson & Jenkins   Piccadilly Circus   London W1A 2AY

Keith A Leonard MD   Fairfax Street   Bristol   BS1 3BO

Grace F Phipps   10 Bridgewater Place   Manchester   M4 8AD

F Chisholm & Co Ltd   High Street   Elgin   Morayshire   IV30 2AA

Technique development

Standard punctuation

Forms of address with punctuation

The guide to the addressing of envelopes, etc., given on page 77 applies with the exception of inserting punctuation after abbreviations and at line-ends. It should be noted that MISS is not an abbreviation and, therefore, there is no full stop after it.

Examples of names and addresses with punctuation

Mr. M. Scott   Rev. C. S. Howe   Messrs. Payne & Sons

```
Miss E. A. McBrien,
Fearnan,
ABERFELDY,
Perthshire.
PH15 2AA
```

```
P. Williams, Esq., M.A., B.Sc.,
56 John Street,
Merthyr Tydfil,
M. Glam.
```

Points to note
(a) A full stop after an initial followed by one clear space.
(b) Comma at the end of each line except for the last line *before* the Postcode which is followed by a full stop.
(c) NO punctuation in Postcode.
(d) Comma after surname followed by one space before Esq.
(e) Use of full stop and NO space between the letters of a degree, but a comma and space between each group of letters.
(f) Notice recognised abbreviation for MID GLAMORGAN.

Practise typing names and addresses with punctuation

1. Type each of the following lines twice. Use margins of Elite 20—80, Pica 11—71.

```
Mr. A. K. Smythe will call to see you next Tuesday at 3 p.m.
Address it to J. Ladd, Esq., M.D., B.A., at 69 Newtown Road.
Miss R. Y. Cruise will meet Mrs. Q. P. Carr at 9 a.m. today.
```

2. Address envelopes to the following. Use block style, standard punctuation, and insert any necessary courtesy titles. Remember to type the post town in capitals.

```
P. F. Stone, M.A., Wessex Close, Basingstoke, Hants. RG21 3NP

Miss A G Watkins 26 Lismore Place Carlisle Cumbria CA1 1LY

Mrs W A Phillips 14 Moorway Lane Littleover Derby DE2 7FS

J Barker & Sons 8 Mill Lane Cheshunt Waltham Cross Herts EN8 9JR

Rev J H Haddington-Davis 23 Daws Heath Road Lewes East Sussex BN7 1AA

Smith & Brown Ltd 124 Easemore Road Redditch Worcestershire B98 8HB

The Victoria Casting Co Ltd 84 Ferry Road Barrow-in-Furness Cumbria
LA14 2PR
```

Further exercise on envelope addressing using standard punctuation is given on page 38 of **Practical Typing Exercises, Book One**

Type the following on A4 paper with margins of Elite 20–85, Pica 10–75. Use double spacing, block paragraphs and shoulder headings. Centre the main heading.

DEMAND FOR FLATS

It wd appear th the market for flats has expanded considerably during the last few yrs, as hundreds hv been & are still being built for sale or to let by private developing cos.

DEMAND

There is a gd demand for flats in residential areas, & the best sellers are said to be those in blocks wh are not more than 3 storeys high.

MARKET VALUE

It is a fact, however, th the value of flats does not increase to the same extent as th of new houses, though new flats hv a higher market value than second-hand ones. Moreover, the sale of the latter generally takes longer.

MORTGAGE

Another hindrance to the sale of flats is th some large bldg socs, who wd be prepared to lend money on a hse, are reluctant to do so for flats.

Type the following on A5 portrait paper, using margins of Elite 12–62, Pica 5–55. Block the main heading at the left margin. Block the first line of each paragraph at the left margin and use hanging paragraphs.

THE RECEPTIONIST

The receptionist is the 1st person a caller wl meet & the impression created is important.

What qualities shd a receptionist hv?   The following are a few suggestions:

(a) Pleasant appearance; dresses attractively & speaks clearly & quietly.

(b) A pleasant disposition & the ability to put people at their ease.

(c) She shd like meeting people.

(d) Courtesy is essential at all times, whatever the provocation. Therefore, patience & self-control, togr w a friendly smile, are ideal qualities.

Type each exercise (A, B and C) three times. Keep your eyes on the copy and return the carriage sharply.

Margins:
Elite 22–82
Pica 12–72

A.   Review alphabet keys

1.   When at the zenith of his power, the tax official began an enquiry into the development of this joint stock company.

B.   Improve control of vowel keys

2. locate unusual receiving suggestion examination distribution

3. assume anxious financial sufficient explanation requirements

4. Your suggestion has been received and we are anxious to have an explanation of your quite unusual financial requirements.

C.   Build accuracy on common prefix drill

5. pro- procure profess process protect promise prolong profile

6. con- contain confirm condemn conceal confess consist contend

7. Promise that you will not prolong the process. Also confirm that Connie will not conceal the contents of that container.

Accuracy/speed practice   30 w.p.m.   One minute   Not more than one error

A/S.42   The weather is likely to remain mild in the south, with   11
some light rain, but in the north there may be slight ground   23
frost, which may lead to icy roads. (S.I. 1.13)   30

A/S.43   The mechanic was not able to fix the valve, and so they   11
had to withdraw their car from the race. The driver did not   23
take part, therefore, in the race. (S.I. 1.20)   30

A/S.44   Conditions have been quite difficult for some time, but   11
we are sure they will improve. We share your view, and know   23
we must be patient and act wisely. (S.I. 1.23)   30

   1 | 2 | 3 | 4 | 5 | 6 | 7 | 8 | 9 | 10 | 11 | 12 |

Record your progress   One minute

R.19   When you have to make up a letter, you should use short   11
words if they express clearly what you want to state. Short   23
sentences are easy to read and help the reader to understand   35
what you wish to explain. (S.I. 1.25)   40

   1 | 2 | 3 | 4 | 5 | 6 | 7 | 8 | 9 | 10 | 11 | 12 |

Opening and distributing the post

1. In some offices all letters are opened before being distributed.
2. In other offices letters addressed to a person or department are *not* opened before being distributed.
3. Letters marked 'Personal' or 'Private' should not be opened before being distributed.
4. Open envelopes carefully with letter opener or with letter-opening machine.
5. Take out letter and first check that *all* enclosures are included. Clip letter and enclosures together. Retain envelope.
6. If an enclosure is missing check that it is not in envelope, and mark letter for immediate attention.
7. Stamp all letters with date, and time of receipt.
8. While date stamping, sort letters into trays or other containers for each person or department.
9. Distribute letters as soon as possible after opening.
10. Registered letters should be entered in special register and signature obtained from persons to whom they are distributed.

Review Quiz No. 3

1. Leave . . . space before and . . . space after decimal point.
2. When typing sums of money in pence only, leave . . . space between figures and the letter p and . . . full stop after p.
3. When typing sums in pounds and pence, use the symbol £ and decimal point but do . . . type the abbreviation . . .
4. If the sum contains a decimal point but no whole pounds, type a . . . after the £ symbol and . . . the point.
5. The decimal point is usually typed . . . the line.
6. Leave . . . spaces between town and postcode and . . . space between the two halves of the code.
7. Turn up . . . single-line spaces . . . and . . . single-line space after the complimentary close before typing the name of company.
8. After the complimentary close, type name of company in . . . . . .
9. Leave . . . clear single-line spaces for signature.
10. The subject heading in a blocked letter should be typed at . . . . . .
11. The attention line is typed . . . single-line spaces below the last line of the address.
12. The last item of an address on the envelope should be the . . . and if this cannot be typed on a separate line it should be typed . . . spaces to the . . . of the last line.
13. . . . full stops or punctuation should be typed between or after the postcode.
14. When matter is to be displayed in columns in a fully-blocked letter, . . . spaces are left between the longest line of one column and the start of the next column.
15. On the envelope the post town should always be typed in . . . . . .
16. Papers or documents to be sent with a letter are indicated by typing the abbreviation . . . , or . . . if more than one enclosure, at the . . . margin at least . . . single-line spaces below designation.
17. In block style all lines of an address start at the . . . . . .
18. In open punctuation . . . punctuation is typed after abbreviations or at the end of each line of the address.
19. . . . space is left between letters of a degree or qualification but . . . clear space is left between each group of letters.
20. A . . . title must always be used with a person's name, but . . . before the name of a limited company, impersonal names or when a . . . is included in the name.

Turn to page 151 and check your answers. Score one point for each correct entry.
Total score: 39

4. Type a copy of the following on A5 landscape paper (210 × 148 mm), making all necessary corrections and typing all abbreviations in full. Use double-line spacing and block paragraphs. Margins: Elite 22–82, Pica 12–72.

SELF-SERVICE STORES

In a self-service store all gds wh are on sale must be plainly on view & the prices clearly marked. It has been found th the more articles wh a customer can inspect, the greater is the value of the sale. Many housewives now go out to work & hv little time to do their shopping, so th the self-service system is a great advantage to them. There are, however, some disadvantages in self-service selling as compared w small shops. The chief one perhaps is the lack of personal touch wh is lacking in supermarkets, & also gds cannot be deld to their customers/ homes.

5. Type a copy of the following on A4 paper (210 × 297 mm), making all necessary corrections and typing all abbreviations in full. Use double-line spacing and indented paragraphs. Set tab stop for paragraph indentation of five spaces.

A changing world → Caps. + underscore

In the world of the 1900ps, electricity was in its experimental stages only. There were not even any electric bell-pushes, bells being operated by a spring. Trams were conveyed to the city by 2 horses w a cabby to drive them. In districts where a steep hill was encountered on the tram route, a third horse was hitched on in front of the others to ease the burden. Life was comparatively simple in those days, nothing but horse trams & horse cabs on the road; one cd take a quiet walk & enjoy the scenery w'out distraction. All the electrical facilities th are now taken for granted - light bulbs, fires, cookers, vacuum cleaners, hair driers, & the rest, were things of the unknown future.

A further exercise on Correction Signs in Manuscript is given on page 29 of **Practical Typing Exercises, Book One**

Skill building

Type each exercise (A, B and C) three times. Keep your eyes on the copy and return the carriage sharply.

Margins:
Elite 22—82
Pica 12—72

A. Review alphabet keys

1.   The expert cricketer, who judged that flight precisely, hit the ball with zest, and very quickly made a large score.

B. Improve control of special characters

2. "2" 3 is/was 4 @ £5 <u>6</u> & <u>7</u> '8' 9 (9 - 8) Mr. & Mrs. one's £12

3. They asked, "Will you <u>both</u> come to Jim's party on March 14?"

4. Mr. & Mrs. Burgess (address below) paid £34 for the antique.

5. He/She requires 20 only @ £5 each, and 18 only @ £5.50 each.

C. Practise line-end division

6. mis-take, com-mand, dis-pose, feel-ing, fic-tion, care-less.

7. suc-cess, mil-lion, con-nect, traf-fic, les-son, sup-ported.

8. home-made, bed-room, trade-mark, under-take, self-possessed.

9. prob-able, chil-dren, knowl-edge, resig-nation, pref-erence.

Accuracy/speed practice	29 w.p.m. One minute	Not more than one error

A/S.37   We hear that you plan to buy some new desks, chairs and 11
files, so we are sending a copy of our price-list which will 23
give you a wide range of choice. (S.I. 1.07) 29

A/S.38   In the spring we always go to a farm, where we are made 11
most welcome. We are allowed to do more or less as we like, 23
and we all have a happy time. (S.I. 1.14) 29

A/S.39   Once a month most firms send to each of their customers 11
a statement of account which shows how much they owe to the 23
firm at the end of the month. (S.I. 1.14) 29

        1 | 2 | 3 | 4 | 5 | 6 | 7 | 8 | 9 | 10 | 11 | 12 |

Record your progress   One minute

R.17   It may be next month before I can be sure of the number 11
of guests we shall have for the Dinner. I feel certain that 23
it will be greater than last year, as members have purchased 35
a hundred or more tickets already. (S.I. 1.26) 42

        1 | 2 | 3 | 4 | 5 | 6 | 7 | 8 | 9 | 10 | 11 | 12 |

UNIT 59

2. Type a copy of the following on A4 paper (210 × 297 mm), making all necessary corrections. Use double-line spacing and block paragraphs. Margins: Elite 22–82, Pica 12–72. Remember to leave an extra single-line space between paragraphs.

<u>CHEQUES</u>

A cheque is an order in writing ~~which is~~ addressed to a bank by a customer directing payment to self or to another person. [There are usually 3 parties to a cheque/ the person who draws the cheque, called the /drawer/, the bank on wh the cheque is drawn, called the "drawee", the person to whom the cheque is to be pd, the "payee".

The main advantage of having a bank a/c is th you can make payments by cheque, thus avoiding the necessity of carrying about w you a large sum of money when you go shopping.

When you make out a cheque, be careful to see th the amt in ~~figures~~ agrees w th written in words. Any alteration made must be initialled by you. [Keep yr cheque book in a safe place at all times.

3. Type a copy of the following on A5 portrait paper (148 × 210 nm), making all necessary corrections. Use single-line spacing and block paragraphs. Margins: Elite 12–62, Pica 5–55.

Trade Descriptions Act ← (Caps + underscore)

Every care is taken to ensure the accuracy of all descriptions + specifications at the time of going to press. We must, however, reserve the right to alter prices as circumstances ~~require~~ dictate with out notice in advance. [Where such alterations in price take place/ customers wl be given the opportunity to amend/ their order.

Similarly, we reserve the right to alter specifications w'out prior notification.

Technique development

Further abbreviations

In typewritten work abbreviations should not, as a rule, be used. There are, however, a few standard abbreviations which are *never* typed in full, and others which may be used in certain circumstances. Study the following list, so that you will know when not to use abbreviations, and when it is permissible to use them.

List of abbreviations always used

e.g. = exempli gratia = for example
etc. = et cetera   = and others
i.e. = id est   = that is
N.B. = Nota bene   = note well
viz. = videlicet   = namely
Esq. = Esquire

Messrs = Messieurs = Gentlemen
          (plural of Mr.)
Mrs.
Per pro (p.p.) = per procuration = by authority of
(used before the name of a person or firm on whose behalf another person signs)

Abbreviations used in certain cases

(a) *Used with figures only:*

* a.m. = ante meridiem = before noon
* p.m. = post meridiem = after noon
  g = gramme(s)
  kg = kilogramme(s)

mm = millimetre(s)
m = metre(s)
km = kilometre
in = inch(es)
ft = foot (feet)

* Note that there is no space between a.m. or p.m.

(b) *Used in cases indicated:*

Ltd. = Limited. Used only in names of companies. (Follow the name printed on letter heading).
Co. = Company. Used only in names. Not in ordinary matter.
O.H.M.S. = On Her Majesty's Service. Usually abbreviated, but sometimes typed in full.
PS. = Postscript. At foot of letter.
b/f = brought forward ⎫ Used in accounts only.
c/f = carried forward ⎭
v. = versus. Abbreviated or can be used in full.
% = per centum. Used only in invoices, quotations, and similar documents.
@ = at, at the price of. Used only in invoices, quotations, and similar documents.
Junr., Jnr. = Junior. Used in addresses (but preferably typed in full).
& = and. Known as 'ampersand'. Used in names of firms, such as Smith & Brown, and in numbers, such as Nos. 34 & 88. Not used in ordinary matter.
Bros. = Brothers. Used only in names of firms.

Practise using abbreviations

1. Type each of the following sentences twice on A5 landscape paper (210 × 148 mm), noting the use of abbreviations. Set margins at Elite 22–82, Pica 12–72. Use block paragraphs and single-line spacing.

Use the abbreviation Ltd. in the name of a limited company.

The book is printed in 3 volumes. Vol. 2 has 600 pages, but Vol. 3 is not so bulky, as it has only 400 pages.

Mr. & Mrs. Browne arrived at 2 p.m., i.e., 10 minutes early.

Mr. Gordon has addressed the parcel to Messrs. Johnson Bros. instead of to Johnson & Co. Ltd.

Further exercises on the typing of abbreviations are given on page 24 of **Practical Typing Exercises, Book One**

Technique development

Simple correction signs

When alterations have to be made in typewritten or handwritten work of which a fair copy is to be typed, or in copy for printers, these are indicated in the original copy by 'Correction Signs'. These signs are recognized and understood by all who are concerned with this type of work.

To avoid confusion, the correction sign is placed in the margin against the line in which the correction is to be made, with an oblique line placed after it to show that it is the end of the particular correction.
Study and learn the use of the following Correction Signs.

Sign in margin	Meaning	Mark in text
l/c or l.c./	Lower case = small letters.	— under letter to be altered or / struck through letter.
u/c or u.c./ or cap./	Upper case = capital letter.	= under letter to be altered or / struck through letter.
Delete (take out).	— through letter or word.
N.P. or //	New paragraph.	[placed before first word of new paragraph.
Stet/	Let it stand, i.e., type the dotted words	.... under words struck out.
Run on/	No new paragraph required. Carry straight on.	
⅄ or L	Caret—insert letter, word, or words omitted.	Placed where the omission occurs. Matter omitted is written in margin.
⌒	Close up—less space.	between letters or words.
trs./	Transpose, i.e., change order of words or letters as marked.	between letters or words, sometimes numbered
#	Insert space.	
	Insert inverted commas.	
	Insert apostrophe.	
	Insert full stop.	
	Insert comma.	
	Insert semicolon.	
	Insert colon.	
	Insert dash.	
	Insert hyphen.	

Practise typing from typescript with simple correction signs

1. Study the following typescript. Then type it on A5 landscape paper (210 × 148 mm) in double-line spacing, making all necessary corrections. Use indented paragraphs, setting tab stop for indentations. Margins: Elite 22–82, Pica 12–72.

PAYMENTS BY CREDIT TRANSFER

Most suppliers agree to payment by this method which is now well known and is used by an ever increasing number of companies. We would like to pay your account in this way and to enable us to do this will you please the slip attached and return it to us at your convenience.

We are always anxious to make prompt payment and thus have the advantage of any discounts that are available to this end will you kindly inform us of your terms for weekly or monthly settlement when returning the authorisation slip in the addressed stamped envelope provided.

Further exercises on typescript corrections are given on page 28 of **Practical Typing Exercises, Book One**

UNIT 62

2. Type the following passage on A5 portrait paper in double spacing. Abbreviations should be typed in full where necessary. Use block paragraphs and margins of Elite 20–60, Pica 10–50.

TRADERS' CREDIT

Normally our suppliers are pd by us by a method wh is known as the "Traders' credit" system, and we shd like y to let us hv yr agreement to our extending this method to yr a/c also. [Under the scheme we instruct our bankers to credit yr a/c w the amt, & y wl rec an advice fr yr banker of the sum credited. [We presume th yr usual discount terms wl still apply, i.e. $3\frac{3}{4}\%$ 14 days or $2\frac{1}{2}\%$ 28 days.

3. Type the following exercise on A4 paper in double spacing. Use indented paragraphs and type abbreviations in full where necessary. Amend the use of words and figures where necessary. Use suitable margins.

DRIVER'S LICENCE

Before y are allowed to drive a motor vehicle, y must pass a driving test wh has to satisfy an examiner th y can handle yr vehicle w safety, whatever the traffic conditions. [The "L" tests were started on 9 June 1935. In that yr 83% of candit: candidates passed. In 1975 the pass rate was 45%. Forty million tests hv been carried out & the demand has risen fr 246,000 in 1935 to 1,621,000 in 1974. The peak yr of tests was nineteen-sixty-seven w a total of 2,010,000. [In 1934 there were 2,400,000 licensed vehicles; in 1974 there were 17,300,000.

Skill building

In exercises A and C, type each line or sentence three times. If time permits, complete your practice by typing each group of lines as it appears. Keep your eyes on the copy and return the carriage sharply.

A. Review alphabet keys

Margins: Elite 22—82
Pica 12—72

1.   Faith quickly jumped over the burning boxes, and walked
away from the scene of the disaster with dazed feelings.

B. Speed up carriage return

2. Type the following lines exactly as shown. Repeat the exercise three times. Keep eyes on copy.

I will.
He will go.
They may go today.
Ask them to go with you.

C. Build skill on word-family drill

3. nip lip hip gip rip tip dip sip van can ban ran pan fan man.

4. bold cold fold hold mold sold told full dull hull bull pull.

5. The man told us that he ran to stop the van as it moved off.

6. He sold a full can of ice-cold orange to that happy old man.

Accuracy/speed practice   29 w.p.m.   Two minutes   Not more than two errors

A/S.40   The rain came down and it was too wet to go out, so the   11
2 boys had to play in the house, and they were quite bored.   23
At last they found a case which had no top, and they planned   35
to make a lid for it, but could not do this without a hammer   47
and nails which they could not find in their tool case.   58
                                                    (S.I. 1.03)

A/S.41   One of the great problems of the present day is noise -   11
noise in the streets, in the home, by day, and sometimes far   23
into the night. Are buses and lorries the chief cause? No.   35
As we hear these all day, we get used to them. So it is the   47
infrequent sounds, such as that made by the jet planes.   58
                                                    (S.I. 1.14)

    1 | 2 | 3 | 4 | 5 | 6 | 7 | 8 | 9 | 10 | 11 | 12 |

Record your progress   Two minutes

R.18   Many people who pay rent are eligible for a rent allow-   11
ance or rebate - an allowance if you are a private tenant or   23
a rebate if you are a council tenant.   30

         You should write to your local council. They will need   41
to know your income. The bigger your family the better will   53
be your chance of getting help, and the sooner you apply the   65
more quickly will you get help. (S.I. 1.36)   71

    1 | 2 | 3 | 4 | 5 | 6 | 7 | 8 | 9 | 10 | 11 | 12 |

UNIT 61   85